If you have ever felt intimidated by the amazing women of the Bible whose stories glow brighter than the gold edges of the pages, *Wicked Women of the Bible* is a breath of fresh air. Oh, not because we can see ourselves—and our failures—in their stories, but because Ann Spangler creatively and carefully helps us see in their tales a God who redeems and repurposes. If you want an in-depth study that will help you be wicked smart about living a life that glorifies God and points others to Jesus, grab a highlighter and experience this lesson-packed book!

*Karen Ehman*

Proverbs 31 national speaker, *New York Times* bestselling author of *Keep It Shut: What to Say, How to Say It, and When to Say Nothing at All*

# WICKED WOMEN OF THE BIBLE

## Other Books by Ann Spangler

*Finding the Peace God Promises*

*The One Year Devotions for Women*

*Praying the Atrributes of God*

*Men of the Bible,*
coauthored with Robert Wolgemuth

*The Names of God Bible* (general editor)

*Praying the Names of God*

*Praying the Names of Jesus*

*Sitting at the Feet of Rabbi Jesus,*
coauthored with Lois Tverberg

*Women of the Bible,*
coauthored with Jean Syswerda

*The Tender Words of God*

**WICKED:** **1.** morally very bad: EVIL **2 a:** FIERCE, VICIOUS <a ~ dog> **b:** disposed to mischief: ROGUISH **3 a:** disgustingly unpleasant: VILE <a ~ odor> **b:** causing or likely to cause harm, distress or trouble <a ~ storm> **4:** going beyond reasonable or predictable limits; of exceptional quality or degree < ~ skill at cards>                    *Webster's Ninth New Collegiate Dictionary*

**WICKED:** very, very good, excellent, extremely, in a grand way; "cool"; "awesome." As in, that concert was wicked!

*The Online Slang Dictionary*

# WICKED WOMEN

# OF THE

# BIBLE

Ann Spangler

ZONDERVAN

*Wicked Women of the Bible*
Copyright © 2015 by Ann Spangler

This title is also available as a Zondervan ebook. Visit www.zondervan.com/ebooks.

Requests for information should be addressed to:
Zondervan, 3900 *Sparks Dr. SE, Grand Rapids, Michigan 49546*

Library of Congress Cataloging-in-Publication Data

Spangler, Ann.
    Wicked women of the Bible / Ann Spangler.—1st [edition].
      pages   cm
    ISBN  978-0-310-34168-0  (softcover)
    1. Women of the Bible—Biography. I. Title.
  BS575.S537  2015
  220.9'2082—dc23                              2015016160

Published in association with Yates & Yates, www.yates2.com.

*Cover design: Tim Green / Faceout Studio*
*Cover photography: Yew Images / Shutterstock®*
*Interior design: Kait Lamphere*

First printing July 2015 / Printed in the United States of America

# Contents

# Introduction

$\mathcal{B}$efore one word of the Bible was ever recorded, its stories and instructions were communicated orally. Though many modern cultures rely heavily on the written word, ancient cultures developed strong oral traditions in which information was handed down from generation to generation.

Certainly that must have been how the stories of the women in this book were first preserved, retold from generation to generation, perhaps around a campfire under starry skies. When the sun went down and their work was done, people shared a meal, recounting the events of the day and then telling the stories of their nation and tribe, regaling each other with memories populated by a colorful cast of characters — real people whom their parents, grandparents, and great grandparents had known.

From their earliest years, children would have thought of the stories of women like Abigail, Bathsheba, and Esther, not as some ancient chronicle, but as part of their own family history. A woman like Esther, for instance, may have been thought of as a cherished aunt rather than as an ancient queen from the distant past.

Some unsavory stories, like the ones about Jezebel or Samson's wicked girlfriend, Delilah, may have been reserved for later, to be told only after the children went to bed. Preserved with remarkable faithfulness because of a strong oral tradition, these and other stories eventually made their way into the Bible we read today.

In *Wicked Women of the Bible* I have done my best to reimagine the stories of some of the Bible's most fascinating women in order to bring them to life for contemporary readers. To do that I've relied on fictional techniques as well as on historical and cultural background information to provide both color and texture. In doing so, I've done my best to stay close to the biblical text, so that today's readers will be able to understand the stories in much the same way as people who listened to them thousands of years ago might have.

One of the things that makes Scripture so believable is that these unsavory stories remain part of it. In truth, the Bible never attempts to clean up the stories or whitewash its characters. Even Sarah, a biblical matriarch whom the New Testament refers to as a holy woman, had her shadow side, wickedly abusing her servant girl Hagar and then throwing her out into the wilderness with no means to survive. And there are far more wicked characters, like Queen Jezebel or Herodias and Salome. If the Bible were merely a puff piece, surely several of these stories would not have made their way into the version we read today.

Why did God put them there? Why did he allow these unpleasant stories to be commemorated? For those who believe Scripture to be the inspired Word of God, these and other stories are in the Bible for a reason. In retelling some of these stories, this book will try to uncover what we can learn by exploring them.

Readers may also wonder why women like Abigail, Esther, and Ruth are included in a book about wicked women of the Bible. My aim has not been simply to highlight the stories of some of the Bible's worst women but also to explore the stories of those who might be considered "wicked good" or "wicked smart."

For anyone who wants to delve more deeply into their stories, I have indicated where they can be found in the Bible. Each story ends with a brief section entitled "The Times," which provides additional background information, as well as a section entitled "The Takeaway," which includes questions designed for individual and group Bible study.

The more time you spend with these and other stories from the Bible, the more you will realize that from beginning to end the Bible is the world's greatest storybook. Whether you are already familiar with its stories or whether you are reading them for the first time, I hope that *Wicked Women of the Bible* will whet your appetite for more, helping you to glimpse the goodness of God and the surprising ways he reveals himself in the pages of the Bible.

As always, it takes a village both to publish a book and to launch it with any degree of success. I am grateful to David Morris, Zondervan's trade publisher, and to associate publisher Sandy Vander Zicht, both of whom enthusiastically supported the idea for this book when they first heard about it. As we discussed the shape it might take, David suggested that it might be interesting to use the word *wicked* in both its literal and ironic sense, an idea I found immediately appealing. As always, Sandy was able to bring her considerable editorial skills and experience to the project, providing guidance that has helped both to shape the book and to improve it in countless ways. I am thankful for her role as friend, encourager, and devil's advocate, a role that every good editor must play. When it comes to editorial help, I am also indebted to Verlyn Verbrugge for the considerable help he has rendered not just for this book but for many of the books I have published over the course of my writing career. Since I am neither a trained theologian or a biblical scholar, I have come to rely on his expertise in these areas to make sure that what I have written is solidly grounded. Thank you, Verlyn, for your careful editorial eye and for the help you have graciously rendered over the course of many years.

On the marketing side, I am also grateful for Alicia Kasen, senior marketing director of Zondervan trade books, and for her creative efforts to spread the word about this book. Gratitude also goes to my agent, Sealy Yates, who caught the vision for this book as soon as I proposed it. I am thankful for his continued efforts on my behalf and for his wise counsel, which I have come to rely on over the course of several years.

Even with the best support an author could wish for, it is likely that there are still weaknesses and deficiencies in the work. Whatever these may be, I take full responsibility for them. Despite the book's flaws, I hope readers will share my enthusiasm for these ancient stories and for the rich insights they continue to reveal to readers today.

CHAPTER 1

# Wicked Lies

---

## THE STORY OF EVE

### How the First Woman
### Swallowed the First Lie

*The heart is deceitful above all things,*
*and desperately wicked: who can know it?*
Jeremiah 17:9

*Bzzt, bzzt.* She swats the flies away, but they keep on coming, too many to count. She has grown used to the constant annoyance, just one of many. Their favorite spot is around her eyes, where they gather to suck the tears away before she has time to shed them.

Still, Eve is a splendid creature, the most beautiful woman in the world, her husband says, enjoying his little joke. She has big honey brown eyes, smooth skin, and thick, dark hair that flows like a river down her back.

Eve has a memory, but it is not long. It swirls about her now, filled with images sharp and bright and shadows deep and long.

She knows what it is like to walk in God's garden, in paths that wind through green meadows and lead to still waters. When she is hungry, she merely reaches out a hand to pick the food that grows in lush abundance. Olives, dates, citrons, almonds, figs, grapes, and pomegranates so big it will take days to eat them.

She recalls what it is like to feel every sense satisfied, every need cared for. To walk with God in the cool of the day. To know the immensity of his love. He tells her she is made in his image. That she and her husband are to rule over the fish of the sea and the birds of the air and over the whole, wide world he has made. They are to be fruitful and multiply so they can care for his great creation.

He speaks to them of how he separated light from darkness and fashioned two great lights — the greater light to govern the day and the lesser light to govern the night. He tells of his delight in placing the stars on their track in the sky. To Eve they look like tiny pricks of brilliant light seeping through the canopy of night.

She listens in wonder as he speaks of how he made a home for her and Adam in the east of Eden, a garden paradise in which all kinds of trees grow — trees pleasing to the eye and good for food. In the middle of the garden grows the Tree of Life and the Tree of Knowledge of Good and Evil.

She remembers, too, what Adam has told her. How God shaped him out of the dust of the ground. He can still recall the hot, sweet breath of God waking his soul to life. He loves to tell about the day God paraded all the animals in front of him — alligators, baboons, gazelles, skinks, parrots, crows, cheetahs, curlews, monkeys, macaws, pythons, bullfrogs, trumpeter swans, yaks, flying foxes, hummingbirds, egrets, elephants, lions, and great, strutting peacocks. God and Adam laughed long and hard as the most preposterous of his creatures passed by. The best part was that Adam got to name them all.

Indeed, Eve knows the scene well, almost as though she had been there, even though God had not yet put Adam to sleep to draw her from his side. Perhaps a memory lingers from when the two had been but one.

Adam always reminds her that even among the most marvelous of the creatures God had made, none was found to be his match. So the Lord God caused him to fall into a deep slumber; and while he was sleeping, God had fashioned a woman from his side.

God's delight was evident when he presented her to Adam and heard him exclaim,

> "This is now bone of my bones
>     and flesh of my flesh;
> she shall be called 'woman,'
>     for she was taken out of man."

This is Eve's favorite part of the story. She loves to hear Adam tell the tale — how stunned he was to meet her. Her breath, he says, smelled like the fragrance of apples, and her breasts were like clusters of fruit. Her mouth was the finest wine.

Eve and Adam. Adam and Eve. The two complete each other. She smiles as she recalls their life together in Eden.

She remembers, too, what she did not know at first — that there could be a place less perfect, a life less loving, a future less bright. That sin could lurk at your door, waiting for a chance to beat you down and shatter you into a thousand jagged pieces, each one a thorn and a barb.

Deceit, blame, want, shame, and terrible grief—all these and worse she has known.

She returns to her memories of what once was. She thinks of all the plants in paradise and of the luscious fruit they bore. The trees were the most delightful. Stately palms, gnarled olive trees, tremendous oaks, and fig trees perfect for playing a hiding game with Adam. But she especially loved the ones that grew in the center of the garden. One of them had bright green leaves lit up with tiny lights that danced inside. The other had deep purple leaves shot through with veins of red.

Why, she wondered, had God told them they were free to eat from any tree in the garden except from the Tree of Knowledge of Good and Evil, warning them that death would surely follow if they did? What exactly was this death he spoke of?

One day, while Eve was thinking such thoughts, and while she and Adam were walking together in the center of the garden, a creature appeared. Not just any creature but one craftier than all the wild animals God had made. The serpent spoke in beguiling tones: "Did God really say, 'You must not eat from any tree in the garden?'" Why, he asked, would a good God deny them anything? Weren't she and Adam the crown of his creation?

For the first time, it dawned on Eve that she might be lacking something, that God might be withholding something vital she needed to know. But she feared such thoughts, and so she merely said, "We may eat fruit from the trees in the garden, but God did say, 'You must not eat fruit from the tree that is in the middle of the garden, and you must not touch it, or you will die.'"

"You will not surely die," the serpent told her. "For God knows that when you eat of it your eyes will be opened, and you will be like God, knowing good and evil."

To know what is good in every situation. To see the end from the beginning and everything in between. To be able to achieve a goal with flawless precision and absolute certainty, surely this was wisdom. Why would God want to keep this gift of power from her?

She turned to Adam as though to find an answer to her silent question, but he said nothing. They were near the tree now. Plucking a piece of fruit, she held it in her hand, delighting in the firmness of its flesh.

When nothing happened, she took a single bite and then another until she had eaten it all.

Then she plucked another piece and handed it to Adam, who ate it without the slightest protest.

Suddenly their eyes were opened, and they could see the wrong in each other's hearts. Ashamed of their nakedness, they sewed leaves from a fig tree to cover themselves.

Then Eve and Adam heard a sound they feared. God himself was walking in the garden. So they hid. "Where are you?" God called.

But who can hide from God?

"I heard you in the garden," said Adam, "and I was afraid because I was naked; so I hid."

Then God, who already knew the answer to his question, inquired of Adam, "Who told you that you were naked? Have you eaten from the tree that I commanded you not to eat from?"

Struggling to explain, Eve's husband spit out the truth, but not the whole truth. He began with an insinuation, blaming God for what he had done. Hadn't God given him the woman? Then he bent the consequences in Eve's direction, saying, "The woman *you* put here with me — she gave me some fruit from the tree, and I ate it."

Then God turned to Eve and said, "What is this you have done?"

The question pierced her like a knife, cutting her heart in two. But she prevaricated, just as Adam had, refusing to bear the blame. "The serpent deceived me," she said, "and I ate."

And then she cowered, her arms above her head as though to ward off blows.

But God merely turned toward the serpent, and said,

"Because you have done this,
Cursed are you above all the livestock
    and all the wild animals!
You will crawl on your belly
    and you will eat dust
    all the days of your life.
And I will put enmity
    between you and the woman,
    and between your offspring and hers;

he will crush your head,
   and you will strike his heel."

But that was not the end of it.
Then God turned to the woman and said,

"I will make your pains in childbearing very severe;
   with painful labor you will give birth to children.
Your desire will be for your husband,
   and he will rule over you."

To Adam he said,

"Because you listened to your wife and ate from the tree about which
   I commanded you, 'You must not eat of it,'
Cursed is the ground because of you;
   through painful toil you will eat of it
   all the days of your life.
It will produce thorns and thistles for you,
   and you will eat the plants of the field.
By the sweat of your brow
   you will eat your food
until you return to the ground,
   since from it you were taken;
for dust you are
   and to dust you will return."

God's words struck like lightning in a sudden storm, flashing across the sky with startling clarity, showing them everything they had lost. The future loomed bleak and harsh before them.

As for God, he was grieved by what had happened, how the man and woman he had loved into being had failed to love him in return. He could not let Adam and Eve remain in the garden he had created just for them. For if they reached out their hand and ate from the Tree of Life, they would live forever in their sin, and there would be no possibility of becoming other than what they were now, broken and bent by sin. So God banished them and placed on the east side of the Garden of Eden cherubim and a flaming sword flashing back and forth to guard the way to the tree of life.

So Eve and her husband were barred from paradise, and the peace they had always enjoyed became like a dream they could barely recall.

They had traded wholeness for brokenness, health for sickness, calm for anxiety, prosperity for want, and harmony for strife. Instead of living in the brightness of God's presence, they lived alone in the dark.

But it was not completely dark. Though Eve and her husband had listened to the biggest lie of all, God had something more in mind for them than punishment. Even so, their lives unfolded just as God had said they would.

Adam named his wife Eve, because she would become the mother of all the living. With great anguish, she gave birth to three sons, Cain, Abel, and Seth. The eldest became a murderer and the second his victim. As for Adam, he labored from morning until evening just to keep his family alive.

And as for God?

Fortunately for Eve and for Adam and for all the children who would become their descendants, God had seen the end from the beginning with everything in between. In his great love, and with absolute certainty, he had set a plan in motion to draw his people back to himself. This bold plan would take uncountable years and face unfathomable obstacles. But sooner or later it would be flawlessly achieved.

Of this Eve was sure, for hadn't God promised that from her would come someone who would crush the serpent's head? In his great wisdom God would provide a way for his children to come home to him.

## THE TIMES

*Her story takes place before recorded time.*
*Eve's story is told in Genesis 1 – 4.*

According to the worldview that prevailed among Israel's neighbors in the ancient Near East, the primary role of human beings was to serve the needs of the gods. They were to do the menial work the divine beings were tired of doing, especially the work of providing food for themselves.

By contrast, Genesis presents God as the one who not only creates the first human beings but who provides food for them by fashioning a garden paradise for them to live in. The garden Genesis describes isn't merely a flower garden or a garden filled with vegetables, but something like a landscaped park with paths, pools, fruit-bearing plants and trees, and life-giving water flowing through it. It was a magnificent garden, the kind that might have adjoined a temple or a palace. The implication in Genesis is that the garden home of Adam and Eve adjoined God's residence in Eden.*

Genesis also makes it clear that men and women, unlike the rest of the living beings God made, were created in God's image. That the gods planted images of themselves on earth would not have been a novel idea. Surrounding peoples believed that these images, which took the shape of idols, monuments, or even kings, were actual images of divinity, containing the gods' essence, which enabled them to do the gods' work on earth.

But Genesis presents only one God, and he is the Creator of everything. Instead of treating Adam and Eve as his slaves, God begins by lovingly providing for their needs and then treating them as his royal image bearers, telling them to "be fruitful and increase in number; fill the earth and subdue it. Rule over the fish in the sea and the birds in the sky and over every living creature that moves on the ground" (Genesis 1:28).

Living in our broken world, it is hard to imagine all that Adam and Eve lost by giving into temptation and transgressing God's clear command. The immediate consequence of their act was to expose their shame. Prior to eating the fruit, they had nothing to hide. But now no amount of clothing could conceal the shadows inside.

---

* For an insightful commentary on Genesis and for more on why the Garden of Eden might be considered part of God's residence in Eden, see John H. Walton, "Genesis," *Zondervan Illustrated Bible Backgrounds Commentary on the Old Testament*, ed. John H. Walton (Grand Rapids: Zondervan, 2009), 1:10–38.

# THE TAKEAWAY

1. Imagine that you are the first woman or man and that you are living in the Garden of Eden. What do you think it would have looked like, smelled like, felt like?

2. In Eden, Eve must have had the perfect relationship with her husband. What do you think that first marriage was like in the beginning?

3. Have you ever disobeyed God because you didn't understand or agree with one of his commandments? What was the result?

4. In what ways would you say the image of God is most broken in people today? How do you think God wants to restore his image in people today?

5. Why do you think God planted Adam and Eve in a garden paradise? What did it say about his expectations for how the first humans were to tend his world, as expressed in Genesis 1:28?

# CHAPTER 2

# Wicked Old

## THE STORY OF SARAH

### How a Ninety-Year-Old Got Pregnant and Set Tongues Wagging

*He that sitteth in the heavens shall laugh.*

Psalm 2:4

$O$lder than dirt. That is Sarah. Her skin hangs like sackcloth, wrinkled and rough. Yet hers is a face that still makes men look, so beautiful it once charmed kings.

You might think her a fool for all the non-stop laughter. Her body shakes with it. But she is no fool, only a woman who can't stop marveling at what God has done. Though her husband is more than a hundred years old and she not far behind, she's pregnant with his child. Who wouldn't find that funny? Two old sticks kindling a fire!

But then it comes — yet another sharp pain snaking down her leg. Ow! The added weight is hard to bear, and loose joints make her wonder whether she will topple over. Though the baby is so ripe she can hardly bend, she never complains. How could she since God Almighty has answered her prayers?

Sarah laughs again, this time because her baby is kicking. He's like a little rabbit whose feet thump softly against her belly. "It won't be long before I hold him in my arms," she thinks.

But how does she know it will be a son?

Sitting in a quiet corner of her tent, Sarah thinks back, remembering all the hurtful things that once were whispered behind her back. She remembers the bitterness she felt every time she heard the women cluck-clucking because God had not blessed her with children. Surely, they would say, Sarah must have done something exceedingly wicked for God to have closed her womb.

Her Egyptian maid Hagar was always the first to throw a stone. She claimed God had cursed Sarah* because she had been unfaithful to Abraham when the two had travelled to Egypt. But what Hagar didn't disclose was that Abraham had asked Sarah to tell a lie to save his skin.

---

* God changed Sarai's name to Sarah and Abram's name to Abraham in Genesis 17 to signify their special relationship with him. For the sake of simplicity I have chosen to render her name as "Sarah" throughout the story.

The couple had fled the parched deserts of the Negev for the lush land of Egypt. Where better to escape a famine than in that place of rich abundance created by the Nile River's frequent flooding?* In Egypt there were plenty of cucumbers, melons, garlic, and fresh fish to eat. But there was also a price to be paid. There always was.

Fearing what lay ahead, Abraham urged Sarah to tell the Egyptians she was his sister lest they decide to murder him in order to have her. And so she recited the lie—but not quite a lie, because Abraham was her half-brother.

As Abraham had feared, word of her beauty spread quickly until Pharaoh declared that he must have her for his own. After showering Sarah's "brother" with gifts of sheep, cattle, donkeys, camels, menservants, and maidservants—of which Hagar was one—clueless Pharaoh added Sarah to his harem.

Before visiting Pharaoh's bedchamber, Sarah had to look the part—to be transformed into an Egyptian beauty. Fortunately, that took time. Anointed with perfume made from precious oils and a crush of fragrant flowers, her face was painted white, its worry lines erased by a potion of cypress kernels, frankincense, wax, and milk. Her dark, curly hair was covered with a black, woolen wig whose braided tresses fell straight to her shoulders. She wore bracelets, rings, and a large necklace made out of gold.

Gazing at herself in a mirror of burnished bronze, Sarah wondered about the woman who looked back at her with so much sadness in her eyes. She had saved her husband's life, but what would happen to her? Would Abraham return home without her? How could she bear to part with him, living out her life as a captive in Pharaoh's harem?

Then something wonderful happened. A swift and terrible plague descended, ravishing Pharaoh's household and leaving only Sarah untouched. The stench of stomachs emptied in a hurry soon flooded the harem and every corner of Pharaoh's house. When he finally rose from his sickbed, Pharaoh summoned Abraham. "What have you done

---

* Geologists and archaeologists have discovered evidence of a three-hundred year drought cycle that took place at the end of the third millennium and the beginning of the second millennium BC, dovetailing with one of the periods in which Abraham and Sarah were thought to have lived. See John H. Walton, "Genesis," *Zondervan Illustrated Bible Backgrounds Commentary on the Old Testament*, ed. John H. Walton (Grand Rapids: Zondervan, 2009), 1:73–74.

to me?" he accused. "Why didn't you tell me Sarah was your wife? You pretended she was your sister. Now your God has cursed me. Take her and go!"

So Sarah and Abraham were hurried out of Egypt and loaded down with all the gifts that Pharaoh could bestow. One of these was Hagar, an Egyptian girl who was to become Sarah's maid.

Hagar has heard the story many times. Indeed, she had lived through part of it. But whenever she recounts the tale, she leaves out the part about God standing up for Sarah, choosing instead to speculate on what it must have been like for her mistress to have become part of Pharaoh's harem.

Sarah knows about her handmaid's tendency to gossip, forever telling half-truths to cast her mistress in a bad light. Why, she wonders, did she ever tell Abraham to sleep with Hagar? At the time, it had seemed like a good idea to invoke the custom of letting another woman provide an heir when she could not. She had hoped it would ease the shame of her own barrenness.

Back then, Hagar had been a slip of a girl, ready to do whatever her mistress asked. Meek and eager to please, she went gladly enough to Abraham's bed. How could Sarah have known that the moment the young woman's belly began to swell with life, she would grow fat with self-importance, behaving as though she, and not Sarah, were the favored wife?

So Sarah began to despise her young maid, making her life a misery. She abused Hagar with words and work until she finally broke. Though pregnant with Abraham's child, the young woman had fled into the wilderness. When that happened, Sarah had felt a momentary twinge of guilt. But then Hagar had come stumbling back with foolish tales of an angel who had persuaded her to return.

Since then, Hagar has been nothing but trouble. How Sarah wishes the wilderness had swallowed her up.

Despite their constant strife, Sarah grows old in the knowledge that her place is secure in Abraham's heart. To know that is something. But it isn't quite everything. Then something happens that makes her realize she is first in God's heart too. Her belly begins to swell with a child. She ignores the wagging tongues and is amused at all the speculation.

How can a ninety-year-old woman survive the birth of a child? Even if she does, how will her shriveled-up breasts produce enough milk? But Sarah is confident. She remembers the promise God made, first in a dream to Abraham, and then last year in broad daylight when he visited them both at their tent near the great trees of Mamre.

That was when the laughter began. Her husband had been sitting at the entrance of his tent in the middle of the day when suddenly he saw three strangers approaching. A generous man, Abraham begged them to linger and enjoy his hospitality. Ducking quickly inside the tent to ask Sarah to prepare some bread, he instructed a servant to slaughter the best calf from his herd.

The moment Sarah completed her task, she began to feel ill. Holding her hand to her stomach, she remembered the long forgotten pain she had experienced whenever her monthly flow began. But that had stopped years ago. Minutes passed until she was certain. She must stay in the tent until her days of uncleanness have passed. Whispering the news to Abraham, she explained why she would miss the meal that was about to begin.

She could see the shock on his face, the worry in his eyes. What woman's disease had she contracted? Would she be able to survive it?

Ever the gracious host, Abraham brought curds and milk and the roasted calf, setting the feast before his guests.

As they spoke, one of them asked, "Where is your wife, Sarah?"

Surely they were wondering why she wasn't at the meal.

"There, in the tent," Abraham replied, invoking a euphemism to explain that, like all menstruating women, she was secluded in her tent.*

Then one of them said, "I will surely return to you about this time next year, and Sarah your wife will have a son." At once, Abraham realized that this was no ordinary stranger. God himself had spoken.

Eighty-nine-year-old Sarah had been listening to the conversation

---

* Though the biblical text (Genesis 18:1–15) never explicitly states that Sarah's period started again, some scholars point out that there is no evidence that men and women ate separately in the ancient world. That was a custom that developed later. So the guests may have noted the irregularity and inquired about it. When Abraham replied that his wife was "in the tent," he may have been employing a polite euphemism, indicating that she was menstruating and unable to join them. For this to have been the case, she would have needed to begin menstruating just after baking the bread because bread baking would have been forbidden to menstruating women. See John H. Walton, "Genesis," 1:91.

from the entrance to the tent. Hearing the stranger's outlandish promise, she broke into laughter, exclaiming to herself, "After I am worn out and my husband is old, will I now have this pleasure?"

"Why did Sarah laugh?" the Lord asked Abraham. "Is anything too hard for the LORD? I will return to you at the appointed time next year, and Sarah will have a son."

Afraid, Sarah replied, "I did not laugh."

Speaking directly to Sarah this time, God said, "Ah, but you did laugh."

And laugh she did and laugh she would until the day her son Isaac—whose name means "laughter"—is finally born. She and Abraham laugh together. The joy rises up strong and wild, and even were she to try, she cannot push it down. "God has brought me laughter," she says, "and everyone who hears about this will laugh with me. Who would have said to Abraham that Sarah would nurse children? Yet I have borne him a son in his old age."

And so it is that in her old age Sarah comes to understand that God has a sense of humor. Despite every shred of trouble and every evil circumstance, she knows that in the end he will prevail, laughing all his enemies to scorn.

But Sarah still has enemies. And they are close at hand.

By now Isaac is three, and he has just been weaned. Since death sweeps so many babies away, his good health is reason to celebrate. Despite the feast that Abraham throws to mark the vigor of his youngest son, Sarah is worried. So she presses him: "Get rid of that slave woman and her son," she tells her husband, "for that woman's son will never share in the inheritance with my son Isaac."

But Abraham's heart is breaking because he loves both sons. How can he deny one to favor the other?

To Sarah's great relief, the Lord appears to Abraham and weighs in on her side, instructing her husband to "do whatever Sarah says." So Abraham sends Hagar and Ishmael packing, straight into the wilderness.

But instead of meeting with ruin, as one might expect them to, they encounter a messenger from God. Because of an angel and a well of water and the Lord's protecting hand, Ishmael grows up and, as the Scripture says, turns into "a wild donkey of a man."

Sarah only knows that she is thankful to be rid of him and Hagar. Finally she can die a happy woman. Of course, she doesn't know that her husband will one day take their son on a three-day journey into the wilderness and then up a mountain to be sacrificed. Abraham will make an altar, place Isaac on it, and then raise his knife to slaughter him.

When Sarah passes at the age of 127, she can imagine neither the glories nor the troubles that lay ahead for the descendants of the two sons of Abraham—the Arabs, who are Ishmael's descendants, and the Jews, who come from Isaac's line.

Had she been able to peer even further into the future, to the time when another beloved son would ascend the very same mountain on which Abraham was told by God to slay his son—she would have come to know the deepest truth of all. No matter how wickedness multiplies or troubles mount up, God will indeed have the last word, laughing his enemies to scorn.

## THE TIMES

She lived around 2156 – 2029 BC.
*Sarah's story is told in Genesis 12:1 – 20; 16:1 – 8; 17:1 – 22;*
*18:1 – 15; 21:1 – 13. She is also mentioned in Galatians 4:22 – 31.*

During the lifetime of Abraham and Sarah, the surrounding peoples worshiped an array of gods. Gradually the concept of a more personal god emerged, with people expressing special devotion to a particular god who would become their special protector and provider. This may have been how Abraham and Sarah first viewed God when they heard him promise to give them many descendants.

Devotion to the family deity would have passed from generation to generation, but other gods would also have been worshiped. Only in Israel would the God of Abraham and Sarah come to be known as the God of the whole nation.

Because the ancient world had so little understanding of what caused diseases and disorders, superstitions abounded, causing additional shame to those who suffered from sickness or physical ailments.

Sarah's grief at being unable to bear children would have been made sharply worse because her barrenness would have been seen as a sign of divine judgment. Surely she had done something to make God angry, and he was exacting punishment by withholding children.

Though ancient peoples would have perceived a connection between menstruation and the timing of a pregnancy, they would not have grasped the biological reality that a human being is created only when a female egg is fertilized by male sperm. They believed that life was created when a man planted his seed into a woman's womb. The woman was seen as a receptacle or incubator in which the seed could grow. If a couple failed to conceive after the man had done his duty, or if the child miscarried, the wife was invariably blamed.

Sarah's barrenness must have put tremendous pressure on her marriage. She couldn't have known that her inability to bear children earlier in life had nothing to do with her sin but everything to do with God's plan to bring about a new people — children of the promise — of whom Abraham would be father and Sarah would be mother. Her pregnancy must have brought a profound sense of vindication and relief.

Four thousand years after her death, Sarah's story lives on. Scripture states that she was buried in the Cave of Machpelah in what is known today as the Tomb of the Patriarchs, along with other key figures whose stories are told in the book of Genesis — Abraham, Isaac, Jacob, Rebekah, and Leah. Located in the West Bank city of Hebron, the site traditionally ascribed to the tomb can still be visited today. It is not far from where Sarah would have sat in her tent, laughing out loud when she first heard God's outrageous promise to give her and Abraham a son.

# THE TAKEAWAY

1. Like many biblical characters, and many real people, Sarah is not an entirely virtuous person. Comment on the good and bad aspects of her character as revealed in the story. Which do you relate to most?

2. Sarah was sixty-five when God promised he would make Abraham (and by inference Sarah) into a great nation. But Isaac wasn't born until twenty-five years later. Why do you think God spoke the promise so far in advance?

3. By suggesting that Abraham sleep with her maid in order to produce an heir, Sarah was merely following the customs of the time. She was also trying to make God's promise come true. Have you ever tried to force God's hand? What were the results?

4. Do you believe God has promised you something? How would you characterize your experience as you waited, and perhaps still wait, for the promise to be fulfilled?

# CHAPTER 3

# A Wicked Disguise

## THE STORY OF TAMAR

### How a Widow Dresses Up Like a Harlot for a One-Night Stand

*For the Lord seeth not as man seeth; for man looketh on the outward appearance, but the Lord looketh on the heart.*
1 Samuel 16:7

*N*ight has fallen by the time Judah and his brothers arrive home, carrying with them the clothing of their seventeen-year-old brother, Joseph. When Jacob sees the richly ornamented robe he had given his favorite son ripped into shreds and covered with blood, the old man wails, "It is my son's robe! Some ferocious animal has devoured him. Joseph has surely been torn to pieces."

Better, Judah thinks, for Jacob to believe his precious son has been eaten by wild beasts than to know the sorry truth—that Joseph is still alive and that he is on his way to Egypt with a caravan of Ishmaelite and Midianite traders* who have paid the going rate for a freshly minted slave.

Despite the fact that Judah has saved his brother's life by suggesting he be sold rather than murdered, as his brothers intended, he is sickened by the whole sorry mess. No matter that Joseph has been such a peacock of a boy and that his father has inflamed the situation by playing favorites. Judah knows it for what it is—a terrible betrayal.

Distancing himself from his grieving father and the wild donkeys who are his brothers,† Judah goes down to the town of Adullam and stays with a man he knows there. Before long he meets and marries a Canaanite woman. Together they have three sons: Er, Onan, and Shelah.

As often happens, one bad decision has led to another. First Judah conspires against his brother Joseph. Then he lies to his father. Then he marries outside his tribe, unlike his forefathers Abraham, Isaac, and Jacob. His marriage opens the door to future difficulties. One of these will come into focus years later, after his eldest son marries a woman by the name of Tamar.

---

* The Midianites were Abraham's descendants through his wife Keturah while the Ishmaelites were his descendants through Hagar. That would have meant that the traders who purchased Joseph and sold him into slavery in Egypt were his second or third cousins.

† Two of Judah's brothers, Simeon and Levi, slaughtered a town full of Shechemite males because one of them had raped their sister, Dinah. For the sordid details, read Genesis 34.

Instead of growing tall and straight, Judah's sons Er and Onan grow like bent branches on the family tree, their ways twisted and deceitful. Their brother Shelah is still a boy, and it is too soon to measure his character.

Er is a sour, weedy-looking man who delights in punishing his wife, Tamar, for his many failings; he is the kind of man others easily overlook. But God does not overlook him. Instead, he notes every detail of Er's wicked ways and arranges for him to make an early departure from this life. At least that's what everyone says when he is found in bed one morning, purple-faced and choking on vomit.

By now Judah has become a man of means. But he is one son short. As is customary, he does the right thing by instructing his second son, Onan, to marry Tamar so that his dead brother may yet have an heir.

Onan is a "yes, Papa, anything you say, Papa" kind of boy. But he has already closed his fist around his dead brother's property as though it belongs to him. Why would he want to sire a son who would eventually snatch it back from him? So he merely plays at being husband. Whenever Onan sleeps with Tamar, he makes sure to withdraw before planting his seed inside her womb. There will be no child.

Tamar says nothing. She is too afraid of what Onan may do to her if she speaks up, and so her tears go unnoticed by her father-in-law, Judah.

But the God who sees everything takes note of Onan's wickedness and puts Judah's second son to death.

Now Judah is two sons short. Who will carry on the line of Judah?

Fortunately, he still has one son in his pocket. But what about Tamar? For a woman to marry a wicked man is tragedy enough. But to marry two wicked men in quick succession — that is more misery than one woman should have to bear. Still, Tamar is willing to hope for better things when Shelah comes of age.

So Judah instructs his daughter-in-law to return to her father's house to live as a widow until Shelah is old enough to marry. But she is uneasy. Why doesn't he let her keep living in his home as is the usual custom? Maybe he thinks she is to blame, her bed accursed. Having lost two sons, perhaps he is unwilling to risk another.

Tamar sits inside her father's house and spends many hours working at the loom. But while her fingers ply the wool, she broods, watching other women do what she longs to. Like hens, they gather their chicks beneath their wings. She wants to watch her own children grow strong and straight so that she can laugh about the days to come. But she has no husband, and there are no sons, and she feels an ache of fear that tells her she has already become the thing she dreads, a widow without a future or a hope.

Time passes and still there is no wedding. Then Judah's wife dies.

One day Tamar catches news of him. He is planning to go up to Timnah for the sheep shearing. Because money is plentiful during the wool harvest, there will be women lying in wait. She knows this. But she is not like them, not in the least.

Tamar trades her plain clothing for a colorful robe and covers her face with a veil. Then she sits down on the road that leads to Timnah and waits.

To Judah, she is a welcome sight. It has not been easy all these months without a wife to comfort him. "Come now, let me sleep with you," he says, his voice beguiling.

"How much will you pay me?" she asks.

"I'll send you a young goat from my flock."

The bartering continues.

"But how can I know you will keep your word? Let me have your seal and its cord, and the staff in your hand."* These she knows are precious to a man.

So Judah agrees and then he sleeps with her.

Later on, Judah sends a friend to deliver the promised goat and to retrieve his property. But the woman has vanished. No one has seen a prostitute† on the road where she was. The answer is always the same: "There's never been a woman like that here."

Judah is puzzled, but what can he do? He never saw the woman's face because she kept it covered by her veil. So he merely shrugs and

---

* Judah probably wore his seal on a cord around his neck. The seal was a stamp or engraving made of stone or metal that could be impressed onto clay or wax. Used to authenticate legal documents, it would have been decorated with a simple picture and may also have included his name. Staffs were often engraved on top, making the owner easy to identify.

† While many translations of the story seem to indicate that Tamar was functioning as a shrine prostitute, i.e., as a woman who engaged in fertility rites, scholars now think that this may be a mistranslation and that the Hebrew word may simply mean "prostitute." So it seems unlikely that Tamar and Judah were engaging in some kind of pagan fertility rite.

says, "At least I tried. Let her keep what she has. If I continue to look for her, the whole world will know about it, and I will become a laughingstock."

Three months pass until a shocking report reaches Judah's ears. "Your daughter-in-law Tamar is guilty of prostitution and now she is pregnant!"

Judah is incensed. How dare Tamar bring shame on his family!

He never considers her circumstances, that she is a childless widow with little means of provision. Nor does he think about what might have driven her to so desperate an act. Instead he thunders judgment, saying, "Bring her out and burn her to death!"

So the best men of the town hurry to do just that. But as they drag Tamar out of her house, she sends a message to her father-in-law along with certain items in her possession. "I am pregnant by the man who owns these. See if you recognize whose seal and cord and staff these are."

Judah is stunned. These can belong to no man but him.

What excuse can he make? The evidence is obvious. He has just condemned a woman for sleeping with a man, but he is that man! So Judah turns in shame to make his own confession: "She is more righteous than I, since I wouldn't give her to my son Shelah."

But that is not the end of the story. Six months later, Tamar gives birth to two babies. During their struggle to enter the world, one tiny arm emerges. Wrapping the baby's wrist with a scarlet thread, the midwife says, "This one came out first." To her surprise, the little hand retreats, and his brother is born instead, prompting her to say, "So this is how you have broken out!"

Tamar's first son is named Perez, which means "breaking out." Her second son is named Zerah, which means "scarlet."

A widow who was all but forgotten by those who should have cared for her, Tamar was remembered by God. Perez grew up and became the father of a stream of descendants who bore delightful names like Amminadab, Abijah, Jehoshaphat, and Zerubbabel. From him also came Boaz, King David, and the wise King Solomon.

As for Tamar, God made her a happy woman by rescuing her from two wicked husbands and then blessing her with two fine sons. As if that were not enough, she is among a handful of women listed in a genealogy in the first chapter of Matthew's gospel. Though their stories are laced with distasteful details, like incest, out-of-wedlock pregnancies, and murder, each woman in the list is remembered as part of a vital chain of human beings that stretches from Abraham to Joseph, the husband of Mary, of whom was born Jesus, who is called the Christ.

## THE TIMES

She lived around 1893–1833 BC.
*Tamar's story is told in Genesis 38.*
*She is also mentioned in Matthew 1.*

The story of how Tamar tricked her father-in-law into sleeping with her so she could become pregnant by him strikes us as both sordid and bizarre. What's it doing in the Bible? Unlike contemporary readers, Jewish people who heard the story would have thought of Tamar as a hero and not as a villain.

They knew that one of the worst fates that could befall a woman was to be without children because a childless widow lacked economic, legal, and social status. When Judah told Tamar to remain a widow even though he had no intention of providing her with a husband, he was breaking the custom of levirate marriage, a common practice in many ancient cultures. To die without an heir was considered a curse. To prevent this, the dead man's wife was married to one of his brothers. Failing that, she could also be married to her father-in-law. Levirate marriage was a way to provide for the widow as well as to produce an heir to carry on her dead husband's name.

An ancient Hittite law read like this: "If a man has a wife, and the man dies, his brother shall take his widow as a wife. (If the brother dies,) his father shall take her. When afterwards his father dies, his (i.e., the father's) brother shall take the woman whom he had."*

Judah was also sinning against Tamar by preventing her from remarrying as other widows would have been allowed to do should the family not provide a husband. Despite her father-in-law's ill treatment, Tamar

---

* Despite the fact that this Hittite law was recorded long after the period in which this story takes place, it captures the law as it may have been practiced at the time of Judah and Tamar. Quoted in John H. Walton, "Genesis," *Zondervan Illustrated Bible Backgrounds Commentary on the Old Testament*, ed. John H. Walton (Grand Rapids: Zondervan, 2009), 1:126.

maintained her loyalty to his family by risking her life to produce an heir. Otherwise, the line of Judah, from whom the Messiah was to come, might have died out. Tamar's actions meant that Abraham's line would continue, not through Judah's wicked Canaanite sons but through the children he had with Tamar.

## THE TAKEAWAY

1. Why do you think the Bible includes sordid stories like this one?

2. Psalm 33:15 says that God watches everyone who lives on earth and considers everything they do. The words of the psalm would seem to be borne out by this story. How does this understanding shape the way you look at what's happening around you? How does it shape the way you look at your own life?

3. What does this story reveal about God's ability to redeem evil even in the midst of entrenched family dysfunction?

4. After condemning his daughter-in-law, Judah realizes his own sin. Have you ever had a similar experience—perhaps while scolding a child? If so, how did you respond?

5. In Tamar's culture, a woman's worth was determined by her ability to bear children, particularly male children. Take a moment to imagine that you are Tamar. You have lost two wicked husbands, the second of which was determined to keep you from having children. Then your father-in-law does the same to you by failing to provide a husband. How do you feel? How would you pray?

6. What kinds of things tend to make you feel worthless? What makes you feel worthwhile?

# CHAPTER 4

# A Wicked Revolt

## THE STORY OF MIRIAM

*For rebellion is as the sin of witchcraft,*
*and stubbornness is as iniquity and idolatry.*

1 Samuel 15:23

*P*apa, tell us the story about Joseph and his beautiful coat," she says. Her dark eyes shine in the firelight, as she leans forward to hear the tale once more. Each time her father recounts it, the story of the young dreamer and his jealous older brothers comes alive in her mind as though it happened only yesterday.

Her father says that God had his hand on the youth from the very beginning, planting dreams of such magnificence inside him that the retelling of them drove his brothers crazy with envy. But even their betrayal could not stop God's plan to make Joseph a great man in Egypt—a man who would save the world—and his own family too.

Miriam knows that Joseph's brothers came down to Egypt, during a time of severe famine. Once in Egypt, they found not only the food they craved but the brother they had sold into slavery years earlier. She remembers Joseph's tears as he revealed himself to his betrayers, and their terror at learning he was still alive. How strange and wonderful that Joseph had forgiven them and settled them and their families on some of Egypt's richest land.

Like them, Miriam lives in the Nile Delta, in Goshen, not far from where the river flows into the Mediterranean. But unlike Joseph, the spirited girl has always been a slave. And yet she dreams of freedom. Her dreams are nurtured by stories about her people that have passed through the generations. They remind her that life has not always been this hard and that there is a God who loves them.

Though Joseph's memory still lives on in the hearts of his people, a new ruler has arisen in Egypt who knows nothing of him. This ruler thinks only of how to control the Hebrew slaves, who are multiplying at an alarming rate. He fears they will soon grow too strong to subdue and that they may conspire with invaders on his northern border. So he decides to cull them, as though they are one of his herds.

He begins by instructing the Hebrew midwives to slaughter every baby boy that's born. But the midwives fear God more than they fear Pharaoh, and so they contrive a lie that only a man would believe. They tell him that the Hebrew slaves are far heartier than Egyptian women. By the time the midwives reach the birthing stool, the baby has already been delivered and hidden away.

So Pharaoh commands his people to throw all the male infants into the Nile River as soon as they are discovered. Miriam thinks it strange that he should try to control her people's fertility by throwing them into the very river he worships as the source of Egypt's fertility.

Miriam's mother, Jochebed, is one of those hearty Hebrew women who has recently given birth to a son. But it is not a cause for celebration, only for worry.

Sometimes Miriam hears screaming in the middle of the night, and she can't keep the tears from rolling down her face. She knows that one more baby has just been fed to the river god.

By now Jochebed's baby is three months old, a lusty boy whose cries might easily give him away. Pressing her cheek to the softness of his, she holds him close and begins to pray. Day after day the words of her prayers rise up like incense to heaven. Hearing them, the great God above — the God of Abraham, the God of Isaac, and the God of Jacob — the God of her fathers looks down with pity and answers.

Suddenly she knows what to do. Pharaoh has ordered every baby boy to be consigned to the waters of the Nile. So be it. Carefully she covers a small papyrus basket with tar and pitch, making certain to coat the surface completely. When she is sure it is seaworthy, she lays her little son inside. His brown eyes gaze at her with so much trust that she is tempted to take him in her arms again and never let him go.

Miriam watches as her mother closes the lid of the waterproof basket and places it into the great river. Her heart is breaking too. How will the baby survive the pythons that lurk on its banks or the hippos and crocodiles that lurk in the water? Standing at the edge of the river, she cranes her neck to see what will happen as the little ark floats away.

Suddenly she spots one of Pharaoh's daughters nearing the river bank. As soon as the princess notices the basket, she sends a slave girl to fetch it. Miriam watches as the girl wades through the water, snatches it up, and then carries the basket to her mistress. She looks on as the princess opens the lid and exclaims, "This is one of the Hebrew babies." How tenderly Pharaoh's daughter lifts his little body from the basket and then holds him against her breast, swaying and cooing to quiet his cries.

Her heart beating wildly, Miriam steps forward to ask if there is anything she can do to help. Perhaps she can find a nurse for the infant. She knows of a Hebrew woman who has just lost a child. She holds her breath to see if Pharaoh's daughter will fall for the ruse.

Fortunately the princess is grateful for her help, and Miriam rushes home to fetch her mother. How convenient, the princess thinks, to have a woman close at hand who has just lost her own child. Could she be the baby's mother? But it's no concern of hers. What matters is that the baby survives.

Thanks to Miriam's boldness and God's unfolding plan, Jochebed is not only reunited with her son but is also paid by a member of Pharaoh's household to care for him. After a few years, when the boy is weaned, he will leave his family and move to the palace. Until then, he is shaped by the love and guidance of his family. Miriam delights him with stories, like the one about Noah and the beasts that climb aboard the ark, or his favorite, the story of Joseph and his jealous brothers.

Time passes and the boy grows strong. One day he walks down a path, holding hands with Miriam and his mother. He knows where they are going. He has always known because his mother is forever singing the princess's praises, telling how she rescued him from the Nile River. He wants to live in the palace but not yet, even though his mother and father say he must. Miriam squeezes his hand, as though to say everything will be all right.

Pharaoh's daughter welcomes them warmly. But when it's time for Jochebed and Miriam to go, the little boy's face contorts with fear, and his arms reach out as though to drag them back. "Don't leave me!" he wails. Miriam turns away, hoping to hide her own fears.

With her arm around Miriam's shoulders, Jochebed leads her out and whispers in her ear, "Hush child, your crying will only make things worse." Then a tear slides down her own cheek.

As for Pharaoh's daughter, she is delighted with her little boy. He will be a fine son, smart and strong. Now that he is safely past the age of weaning, she gives him a name. He will be called Moses, she says, "because I drew him out of the water." And so she had.

So Moses, a boy whom Pharaoh had tried to murder, grows up right beneath his nose, living in his palace, putting his feet up, eating his food, and getting the best education Egypt can provide. Whenever Miriam thinks of this, her pain eases. She laughs a little because it proves that God is in control and that he has a sense of humor.

Years pass. By now Moses is a grown man—forty years old. He is tall and broad—the picture of Egyptian dignity and power. Miriam wonders if he still remembers her. She hopes he recalls the stories she told him about a mighty God who had chosen their people and promised them a land to live in. Perhaps he will find favor with Pharaoh and become the one to lift them out of slavery, saving his family as Joseph did.

But this dream of hers, that God will deliver the lowly ones who cry out to him day and night, all but vanishes when she hears that Moses has been accused of murder and that Pharaoh intends to kill him as soon as he can lay hands on him. What is his crime? He has slain an Egyptian slave driver who was beating a slave to a bloody pulp.

Moses escapes, and she hears nothing of him for forty years.

After a while the king of Egypt dies, and another Pharaoh ascends the throne. This one, they say, is worse than the last, with the heart of a viper. A tiny, golden cobra—the emblem of Wadjit, the protective goddess of the Delta region—adorns his crown, reminding his enemies of his strength and cunning. It proclaims his power, as though to say he will surely strike should anyone be fool enough to challenge him. With Wadjit's protection he feels his throne secure.

But Pharaoh's smugness would vanish quickly if he perceived the truth—that even now a Deity he does not know is stirring up trouble, calling forth a deliverer who will marshal the forces of nature to wreak havoc on his kingdom. It has been in the Lord's mind from the start, when he brought Moses to life in his mother's womb and then kept him alive with the help of Miriam and Pharaoh's daughter.

But where has Moses gone? By now he is living in the desert of Midian, east of Egypt. It is a place where God can shape and mold him into the man he must become, because there are some things that only the wilderness can teach.

One day, as Moses is tending his flock near Mount Horeb,* God appears in the shape of a burning bush. Out of the fire he speaks a harrowing word:

"Moses, Moses! Take off your sandals, for the place where you are standing is holy ground. I am the God of your father, the God of Abraham, the God of Isaac and the God of Jacob....

"I have indeed seen the misery of my people in Egypt. I have heard them crying out because of their slave drivers, and I am concerned about their suffering. So I have come down to rescue them from the hand of the Egyptians and to bring them up out of that land into a good and spacious land, a land flowing with milk and honey. So now, go. I am sending you to Pharaoh to bring my people the Israelites out of Egypt."

Shielding his face with both arms, Moses is afraid to look into the flames lest he see the face of God and die.

Somehow he finds the courage to respond. "Since I speak with faltering lips, why would Pharaoh speak to me?" But the Lord assures him he is perfect for the job, not because he is strong or persuasive. He is neither of these. But because God himself will be with him.

When Moses returns to Egypt after an absence of forty years, he meets his family again. Though his parents are dead, his bond of love with Miriam and Aaron is renewed. The three take counsel together and then meet with the elders of Israel, and all concur: he and Aaron, who is to be his mouthpiece, are to go to Pharaoh and tell him what the Lord has said—that he must "Let my people go."

So Moses meets with Pharaoh, but Egypt's arrogant ruler merely puffs up his chest and scoffs. "Who is this Lord you speak of?" He lingers on the word *Lord*, drawing it out as a deliberate mockery. "I do not know him, and I will not let Israel go." His arms are folded; his jaw is set. Then he accuses the slaves of laziness and doubles their workload.

Exhausted, many of the people curse Moses, accusing him of making things far worse with all his foolish talk of freedom. Miriam has always known that the struggle for freedom would be hard. But she never expected the challenge that now comes from within her own community.

---

* Also known as Mount Sinai.

But Moses and Aaron won't give up, and so they return to Pharaoh's court. Aaron throws down his staff, and it transforms into a snake. Pharaoh tries to hide his surprise. Surely, he thinks, this is only a bit of trickery. So he calls on his sorcerers to see if they can match the trick. Remarkably they do, throwing down their staffs and watching as the floor becomes a nest of writhing, hissing snakes.* But before he has time to gloat, he watches as Aaron's staff devours every single one of their staffs.

The magicians step back. The sign is unmistakable. The God of Moses and Aaron has challenged and defeated the goddess Wadjit, whose emblem is the snake — the cobra on Pharaoh's crown. Pharaoh, too, is shaken. Without Wadjit's mystical protection, how can his kingdom stand? But his heart is as hard as flint, and he will not let God's people go.

So the battle continues with plague upon plague upon plague. The Nile turns to blood, the land teems with frogs, the dust turns to gnats, great swarms of flies invade the land, the livestock is struck down, festering boils break out on beasts and humans alike.

In the midst of these horrors, Miriam feels her hope rising like sap in a tree. She knows God is at work to free his people and that she must help them get ready for their journey out of Egypt. It could happen any day.

More plagues follow. Hail beats down the vegetation, locusts devour what remains, darkness covers the earth and — worst of all — the beating heart of every firstborn son in Egypt is stilled, and there is mourning and wailing and grief such as the nation has never known. It has happened just as God and Moses said it would. Only the land of Goshen, where God's people live, is spared.

Finally, in the middle of the night, when the Egyptians are counting their dead, Pharaoh summons Moses. "Up! Leave my people," he cries, "you and the Israelites! Go, worship the Lord as you have requested. Take your flocks and herds, as you have said, and go."

In their haste to be rid of their former slaves, the Egyptians shower them with gold, silver, and fine clothing as though they have just been plundered by a conquering army.

---

* Snake charming was practiced in ancient Egypt by magicians who knew tricks that would put their snakes into a rigid, trance-like state. See "The Egyptian Priests and Their Snakes," in *The Archeological Study Bible*, ed. Walter C. Kaiser Jr. (Grand Rapids: Zondervan, 2005), 96.

So Moses, Miriam, and Aaron and all the ragtag band of Hebrew slaves and anyone else who wants to leave Egypt begin to march out. The women are adorned with beautiful rings, necklaces, and golden bracelets reaching from wrist to elbow. The men are weighed down by pouches filled with silver. The children skip and play, oblivious to the dangers of their new adventure.

The great crowd of slaves go out from the land of their captivity singing and dancing, but not at first, because Pharaoh makes a last, brainless attempt to overtake them in their march to the sea.

On they come, the chariots. Great clouds of dust mark their passing, and the people begin to panic. "We will be swallowed up," they cry, "trapped between the sea and Pharaoh's chariots!" Miriam and Aaron try to hold the line, to put a lid on the panic while Moses tells the people, "Do not be afraid. Stand firm and you will see the deliverance the LORD will bring you today. The Egyptians you see today you will never see again. The LORD will fight for you; you need only to be still."

Then Moses stretches out his arms, and all that night the Lord holds back the Egyptian pursuers while he unleashes a strong east wind to uncover the floor of the sea so that the Israelites can march across.

A horde of people — young and old — along with all their herds, march through the open trench with walls of water piled on either side. With the deafening wind still beating back the waves, Pharaoh reaches the water's edge and urges his chariots forward, anticipating the slaughter he will soon wreak upon his fleeing slaves. But his chariots become mired in mud, and their wheels fall off. By the time he realizes his mistake, it is too late to turn back.

With God's people now safely across, Moses lifts up his hands again, and the walls of water collapse on Israel's enemies. Every soldier, every horse, every chariot is smothered beneath the waves of the angry sea, forever buried in a watery grave.

Then Miriam takes a drum* and begins to lead a great, wild dance of victory as her people reenact the battle God has just won. Her skirt swirls and swings as she dances and sings a song that will never be forgotten.

---

* Though the biblical text translates the scene as though Miriam is playing a tambourine, scholars indicate that the tambourine had not yet been invented. More probably the text is referring to a hand drum of some kind. See Miriam Feinberg Vamosh, *Women at the Time of the Bible* (Nashville, TN: Abingdon, 2007), 66.

Sing to the LORD,
>for he is highly exalted.
Both horse and driver
>he has hurled into the sea.

Then Moses along with Aaron and Miriam lead the people forward on their long and arduous journey through the wilderness. And as they march, God speaks. Sometimes he comes to Miriam in visions and dreams. She is a prophet, a woman he entrusts with divine guidance and words of wisdom.

One day she and Aaron begin to murmur. The people are difficult to lead, the journey longer than they had envisioned. Why does Moses make all the decisions? Hasn't God spoken through them too? Their complaints mount up and spill over, and they begin to criticize him publicly for taking a foreign wife.* But that is merely a pretext. What they want is power, a bigger role to play. And the Lord hears them speaking against his servant Moses.

At once, God summons the three of them and has them stand before him. He calls Miriam and Aaron forward. "Listen to my words," he thunders from the pillar of cloud that hovers above the tabernacle.

"When there is a prophet among you,
>I, the LORD, reveal myself to them in visions,
>I speak to them in dreams.
But this is not true of my servant Moses;
>he is faithful in all my house.
With him I speak face to face,
>clearly and not in riddles,
>he sees the form of the LORD.
Why then were you not afraid
>to speak against my servant Moses?"

God's anger burns against them both, and when the cloud lifts, there stands Miriam — covered with white scales. She is leprous like snow.

Horrified by what has happened to his sister, Aaron begs Moses to pray: "Please," he says, "ask God to lift the curse." Since Moses is more humble than anyone else on the face of the earth, he does what Aaron asks, crying out to the Lord, "O God, please heal her!"

---

* Moses married a Cushite woman prior to returning to Egypt in order to deliver his people from slavery.

And God replies with words that burn in Miriam's heart: "If her father had spit in her face, would she not have been in disgrace for seven days? Confine her outside the camp for seven days; after that she can be brought back."

So Miriam is healed and forgiven but not before she is exiled for seven days. During her confinement, she has time to reflect on the wickedness of what she and her brother Aaron have done. It is true that God has spoken to her. He has made her a leader and a prophet. But she is not Moses. She had not been drawn out of the waters and raised in Pharaoh's household. She had not met with God face to face as her brother had done.

She remembers the story of Joseph and his jealous brothers, and as much as she dislikes the thought, it occurs to her that she, too, has lost a fight with jealousy. She has been so blindly jealous that she did not realize she and Aaron were risking her people's future by challenging Moses and the words God spoke through him.

But why was Aaron not punished too? Perhaps because God in his wisdom did not want the worship of the tabernacle to be disrupted by Aaron's absence as high priest.

After seven days, a mild punishment she thinks, Miriam is restored to the community, and the people set out once again. After forty years of wandering and many difficult adventures along the way, God's people finally approach the land of promise. But Miriam will not reach it, nor will Aaron, nor will Moses. All three will die before they can enter the Promised Land.

So the people mourn them as they stand on the brink of taking hold of God's great promise to give them a land flowing with milk and honey—a paradise all their own. The task of leading them all the way in will fall not to Moses but to Joshua, a warrior who can safely guide them through all the battles that lie ahead.

# THE TIMES

Her story probably takes place from about 1533 BC to 1406 BC.
*Miriam's story is drawn from Exodus 2 – 3; 5; 7:*
*1 – 13; 12:3 – 36; Numbers 12.*

Though it's not possible to pin down the exact time of the exodus, it seems clear that Israelites were at one time enslaved in Egypt. Unlike the Egyptians who worshiped as many as 1,500 gods throughout their history, the Israelites worshiped only one God, whose name is *Yahweh*.

It is only by listening to Yahweh and heeding his direction that Moses is able to lead the Israelites out of Egypt. And it is only by following Moses' leadership that Miriam, Aaron, and the people will survive the wilderness.

The battle between Moses and Pharaoh is an epic one that symbolizes the battle between good and evil. It is a battle not merely between humans but between God and all the false gods of the Egyptians who had enslaved his people.

Even today, the exodus story shapes the understanding of both Jews and Christians who believe that each of us can identify with the story in a personal way. Just as the Israelites were in bondage to Pharaoh, who personifies evil, we, too, are beset by evils, from which only God can deliver us. If we follow him, he will lead us out of bondage and into a life of freedom.

Though Miriam is struck by "leprosy" for opposing her brother, there is little evidence of what we call Hansen's disease in the ancient Near East. The Hebrew term that is translated as "leprosy" probably refers to diseases like ringworm, psoriasis, or eczema.

As is often the pattern in Scripture, God uses unlikely heroes in unlikely ways to accomplish his purposes. Though Moses and Aaron stand against Pharaoh, it is God himself who does the fighting. This epic battle, like all spiritual battles, cannot be won by human strength but only by God's power.

# THE TAKEAWAY

1. Imagine that you are one of the women who played a pivotal role in saving Moses—a Hebrew midwife, Jochebed, Miriam, or Pharaoh's daughter. What goes through your mind and heart as you confront the circumstances?

2. How has God worked in your own life to deliver you from evil?

3. People who have never been there often think of Egypt as a vast desert, failing to understand the lushness of the land around the Nile River. The first forty years of Moses' life were spent in a fertile landscape. Why might God have allowed him to spend the next forty years in the desert before choosing him to lead his people for forty more years through the wilderness?

4. Moses first encountered God at Mount Horeb, also known as Mount Sinai. Instead of leading the Israelites on a straight path to the Promised Land, God led them first to the holy mountain, where they encountered him and received his commandments. Comment on the significance of this.

5. What adjectives would you use to describe Miriam? In what ways are you like her? In what ways are you unlike her?

# CHAPTER 5

# A Wicked Woman of the Night

## THE STORY OF RAHAB

### How a Shady Lady Tells a Lie and Saves the Day

*Know therefore that the LORD thy God, he is God, the faithful God, which keepeth covenant and mercy with them that love him and keep his commandments to a thousand generations.*

Deuteronomy 7:9

*W*henever she walks to the market, the women gather in little knots, shutting her out while the children snigger and point. But she just tosses her hair and swings her hips, provoking them all the more.

They are jealous, she thinks, because she makes a living that's five times better than theirs. Plus their husbands give her looks that tell her they are wondering what it would be like to caress her honey-gold skin and run their fingers through her thick, curly hair. The women retaliate by wagging their tongues. Their words are like little slingshots filled with insults.

But Rahab doesn't care. She has the best of everything. A thriving business, good health, a quick wit. Plus she likes breaking molds. Surprising people. An enterprising woman, she owns a home, an inn* really, that fits snugly inside the city's impenetrable walls. Because of its location near the city gate, she misses nothing, sees everyone as they pass through. Travelers from all over the region carry news of the world beyond. No wonder the king of Jericho sends his emissaries to her from time to time to gather the latest intelligence.

Some of her guests are only looking for a bed, while others want to share hers. On the side, she works in linen, retting the long stalks of flax and then laying them out on the rooftop to dry before their soft fibers can be extracted and spun into thread. Today, though, it is not thread she's spinning but dreadful visions drawn from all the rumors she is hearing. What will happen to her parents, her brothers and sisters, and all their children if the tales are true?

Visiting merchants who are part of large caravans that crisscross the region are buzzing about the presence of a great horde of people encamped at Shittim, ten miles to the east of Jericho, on the other side of the Jordan River. Rahab has heard the stories — how the Israelites

---

* The term for "prostitute" may also have meant innkeeper. In that era innkeepers were often associated with prostitutes.

left Egypt in triumph, and how their God reached down and parted the waves so they could walk across the sea to freedom. She knows these former slaves have been toughened by forty years in the wilderness, and that they are fed with a mysterious food called manna. Perhaps that is what has made them so strong. Already they have annihilated the Amorite kings, Og and Sihon. Everyone says Jericho will be next.

But Jericho has survived the ravages of millennia. How can the world's oldest city possibly be conquered? Its walls are stout and tall, impossible to scale. Yet, still, its people tremble, and great waves of fear assail them as each new story builds upon the last, telling of the prowess of Israel's wonder-working God.

Like everyone else, Rahab is afraid. But her fears can't crowd out her curiosity. How is it that a band of slaves who lived in Egypt for more than four hundred years have slipped their bonds and become a mighty army? And why do they worship only one God, a God who speaks to them from a pillar of cloud by day and a column of fire at night?

Oh that she might know the protective power of such a God. That he might hold her in his all-sheltering arms and keep her safe.

But now night is drawing near—the busiest time of her day. Two strangers have just arrived, and something in the shape of their faces and the cut of their beards puts her on the alert. She is used to foreigners but not to men like these. Their skin is dark and weathered, their eyes bright and full of a singular purpose.

"You are Israelites!" she exclaims.

They try to hush her but don't deny it. In an instant she chooses sides. "Come with me," she says.

Leading them to the rooftop where long stalks of flax lay drying, she instructs them to hide beneath them.

Moments later, other visitors arrive. She opens the door a crack to see the king's men standing outside. "Bring out the men who are staying at your house," they demand. "They are spies."*

Her fingers clutch her throat in feigned surprise, as though to say she

---

* The Code of Hammurabi (a set of laws in Mesopotamia that date back to about 1772 BC) states: "If there should be a woman innkeeper in whose house criminals congregate, and she does not seize those criminals and lead them off to the palace authorities, that woman innkeeper shall be put to death." Quoted in Richard S. Hess, "Joshua," *Zondervan Illustrated Bible Backgrounds Commentary on the Old Testament*, ed. John H. Walton (Grand Rapids: Zondervan, 2009), 2:19.

is alarmed to learn she may be sheltering spies. "Two men were here," Rahab answers, "but I didn't know who they were. They left the city at dusk, just before the gate closed. I have no idea where they've gone. If you leave now, you may still be able to catch them."

The men assume that the shake in her voice comes from fear at discovering that an enemy has come so close. When they are gone, she moves to the window and notes their route as they head in haste toward the fords of the Jordan River.

Then she steadies herself and heads up to the rooftop to alert her guests. She says to them, "I know that the LORD has given this land to you and that a great fear of you has fallen on us, so that all who live in this country are melting in fear because of you. We have heard how the LORD dried up the water of the Red Sea for you when you came out of Egypt, and what you did to Sihon and Og whom you completely destroyed. When we heard of it, our hearts melted and everyone's courage failed because of you, for the LORD your God is God in heaven above and on the earth below.

"Now then, please swear to me by the LORD that you will show kindness to my family, because I have shown kindness to you. Give me a sure sign that you will spare the lives of my father and mother, my brothers and sisters, and all who belong to them, and that you will save us from death."

"Our lives for yours!" the men assure her. Then they instruct her to tie a scarlet cord in her window so that the Israelites will recognize her house when they invade the city. No matter what happens, she is to make sure that every member of her family — from the youngest to the oldest — stays put inside the house. Even a moment outside could mean their deaths.

Agreeing, Rahab lowers the spies by rope from her window, telling them to hide in the hills for three days.

When the two men finally arrive at Shittim, they tell Joshua everything and watch as a smile spreads across his craggy face. "Surely," he says, "the LORD himself has flooded Jericho with fear." As Moses' successor, he will trust God for the victory. Though Joshua has no idea how he and his men will scale the walls of Jericho, he rallies his people, and they march until they arrive at the eastern banks of the Jordan River.

In the summer the river is only a trickling stream, but in the spring-time it runs fast and high. A strong man might make it across, but everyone else will perish. Even so, Joshua tells the priests to take up the ark of the covenant, which is a pledge of God's presence, and carry it into the river.

The priests are certain they will be swept away, except for one thing. God is going into the river with them. Though only boys when they left Egypt, they remember how God made a way through the Red Sea when they were trapped by Pharaoh's advancing army. Now they have become a mighty army advancing into the land God promised them. So they do exactly as Joshua says.

As soon as their feet touch water, the river stops flowing and the ground begins to dry up. Slowly they advance, carrying the ark into the middle of the riverbed. Standing there, hour by hour, they wait until every Israelite has crossed. Then they walk in procession to the other side. As soon as they and the ark stand safely on the river bank, the water rushes back and the river becomes as it was.

Now they are only five miles from Jericho.

A few days pass. God speaks to Joshua again, and he does exactly what God says.

Meanwhile, within the city walls of Jericho, no one goes in and no one goes out. There is too much fear. Panic has gripped the city because everyone has heard how the Israelites have miraculously crossed the Jordan.

By now Rahab's house is crowded with relatives. She watches from the window as the Israelite army marches toward the city. Instead of rushing the walls, they parade around them, carrying a golden box that glints in the sun. On top of the box sit two golden angels facing each other, their wings extended as though to shelter it. Carried on long poles, the sacred box is preceded by seven priests who blow seven ram's horns. Not a single word is spoken as the Israelites march around the city. Rahab hears only the tramping of feet and the blowing of horns. After the soldiers parade around Jericho once, they return to the Israelite camp.

No one knows what to make of this strange procession. It is not what the citizens of Jericho expected.

The same thing happens the next day and the day after that. For six days the Israelites march around the city carrying their beautiful golden box. If they meant to terrify Jericho's inhabitants, they have succeeded. Many people can no longer stand the sound of the blowing horns.

But Rahab is not one of these. Instead of terror, she feels strangely calm. Each time the golden ark passes by, she senses a presence that gives her peace.

On the seventh day, instead of processing around the city once, the Israelites keep on marching. They encircle the city seven times. On the seventh pass, when terror has built to a crescendo, a great shout goes up from all the Israelites. It goes on forever like a rolling wave of sound that will smash the world to bits. All at once, the encircling walls collapse. Rahab's small house tilts, cracks, and pitches slightly forward, but it does not fall. She prays that the spies will keep their word.

As she sits inside her house, she hears a great clash of weapons and screams that chill her heart. The city is quickly overwhelmed and then burned to the ground. Of all who lived inside its walls, only she and her family are spared.

Like Noah and his family, Rahab and her people escape the great destruction that comes as punishment for the sins of those who live in the land. Instead of a boat, it is a house that shelters them. Because Rahab believed in Israel's God and risked her life to help his people, she and her family are saved.

Had anyone from Jericho been able to tell the story, her role would have been described not with words like *courage* and *faith*, but with words like *treachery* and *deceit*. As it is, not one person was left alive who could contradict the story as it has been handed down through all the generations of God's people.

Leaving the ill-fated city behind, Rahab and her family settle with the Israelites. One of her descendants will be David, the greatest of Israel's kings. More remarkable than that, she will be known to later generations as the great, great, great-beyond-counting grandmother of Jesus, who is the Christ.

# THE TIMES

Her story may have taken place about 1406 BC.
*Rahab's story is told in Joshua 2 – 3 and 6. She is mentioned*
*in Matthew 1:5; Hebrews 11:31; James 2:25.*

Jericho was a fortified city, with perhaps as many as two thousand residents. Also called the "City of Palms," it was located along important trade routes, just fifteen miles from Jerusalem. Archaeological evidence for its existence dates to the ninth millennium BC, which may make it the oldest city in the world.

Prior to advancing against Jericho, the Israelites celebrated Passover by eating some of the produce of the land. The next day, the manna that had nourished them throughout their wilderness journey stopped because they no longer had need of it (Joshua 5:11 – 12).

When the Israelite spies reached Jericho, they realized that God was already at work within the city to weaken it, spreading "a great fear" of them, as Rahab told them.

It was springtime when Joshua led the people across the Jordan River, a time when the river was at flood stage. The Bible says that "the water from upstream stopped flowing. It piled up in a heap a great distance away, at a town called Adam" (Joshua 3:16). Jericho is located in the Rift Valley, an unstable region with frequent seismic activity. It is possible that an earthquake caused the high banks of the Jordan to collapse upstream from where the Israelites were crossing, damning up the river. In 1997, an earthquake in the vicinity of Adam dislodged a 150-foot-high embankment, which stopped the flow of the river for twenty-one hours. The walls of Jericho may have collapsed because of a second earthquake, which could have enabled Joshua and his men to breach the city's defenses.[*]

But how could Rahab's house have survived an earthquake? Excavations in the early twentieth century have revealed a portion of the lower city wall that did not collapse. Houses that were built against it were still intact.

---

[*] See "Crossing the Jordan" in *The Archeological Study Bible,* ed. Walter C. Kaiser Jr. (Grand Rapids: Zondervan, 2005), 306.

# THE TAKEAWAY

1. There are striking similarities and some differences in the way the Israelites began and ended their forty-year sojourn in the wilderness. Both involved a miraculous crossing of impassable water. Both occurred near the celebration of Passover. In the first case, Israel was being pursued. In the second, they were the pursuers. How do you account for the similarities and the differences?

2. The Israelite priests had to step into the Jordan before it stopped flowing. Have you ever acted simply on the basis of your trust in God, taking a risk before experiencing the answer to a prayer or the fulfillment of a promise? If so, what were the results?

3. The command to march around Jericho seven times must have sounded bizarre to Joshua. How might the story have changed had he disobeyed God and relied on his own battle strategies? What are the implications for our own lives as people of faith?

4. To many of us, the annihilation of every living creature in Jericho sounds cruel and inhumane. But Scripture portrays the conquest of Canaan as a judgment against the sins of the people in the land. Among other things, the Canaanites were said to have practiced child sacrifice. Do you think God judges people in similar ways today, by bringing destruction to their lives? Why or why not?

5. Rahab was willing to risk her life to protect the spies. What kind of risks have you taken that express your trust in God?

6. In Exodus, Moses is the hero who grows up right under the nose of his enemies. In this episode from the book of Joshua, God uses Rahab as the "insider" who will help his people overcome their enemies. What does this say about God's ability to work on behalf of those who belong to him?

# CHAPTER 6

# A Wicked Surprise

## THE STORY OF DEBORAH AND JAEL

*God hath chosen the weak things of the world
to confound the things which are mighty.*

1 Corinthians 1:27

$\mathcal{D}$eborah can't remember a time when she didn't pray. As a child, not praying would have been like not skipping across the fields or not picking wildflowers in spring or not laughing at a good joke. An impossibility.

She asked God to make her beautiful and strong and smart enough to please her father and outwit her brothers. She prayed that God would bless every baby born from her mother's womb and that their home would have less shouting and more kindness. She prayed that even the most witless of their sheep would behave whenever she was charged with watching over them.

She learned to thank God for every answered prayer. And as she grew, God taught her to thank him even for what she liked the least—the times when he said no.

One prayer he hadn't answered was to make her beautiful. But now that she has grown up, her huge brown eyes and the calm that radiates from them draw people close. They trust her.

Her husband knows he has found a treasure. For she has brought him good all the days of his life. Her wisdom has helped increase his wealth and added to his reputation. He feels like laughing whenever he thinks of his good fortune. How is it that he, an ordinary man, has found a woman who is clothed with so much strength and dignity? A woman who loves him more than she loves herself and whose wisdom has become legendary?

Every day Deborah sits beneath a large date palm to meet with her people. They come seeking a word from God. Will the rains come early or late? Is God pleased with my sacrifice? Will my wife have a child? Am I right and my neighbor wrong? Will I recover from this illness?

Deborah knows her people are not strong and that many of them are hounded by troubles. Some seek her as though she is a soothsayer who is able to beguile the gods to do her will. But she believes in only

one God, the God of her ancestors—of Abraham and Sarah, of Rahab
and Joshua. Hers is a God who rides across the highest heavens, the
ancient heavens, a God who thunders with a voice that even the wind
obeys. She hears his voice regularly, sometimes in thunder, more often
in silence.

It has been nearly two hundred years since the walls of Jericho were
breached and the city burned to the ground. Though Deborah's people
swept into Canaan like an unstoppable force, they failed to drive out all
the peoples who lived in the land.

There had been too much sin for that. Too much weakness.

Bowing down to the Baals of Canaan, who promised them fertile
fields and a quiver full of children, they had forgotten the ways of the
God who delivered them out of the hand of wicked Pharaoh. It has
been like this ever since Joshua and the generation that followed him
died off. Their children and their children's children have forgotten
Joshua's stern warning.

"Be very strong; be careful to obey all that is written in the Book of
the Law of Moses, without turning aside to the right or to the left. Do
not associate with these nations that remain among you; do not invoke
the names of their gods or swear by them. You must not serve them or
bow down to them. But you are to hold fast to the LORD your God, as
you have until now.

"The LORD has driven out before you great and powerful nations;
to this day no one has been able to withstand you. One of you routs a
thousand, because the LORD your God fights for you, just as he promised. So be very careful to love the LORD your God.

"But if you turn away and ally yourselves with the survivors of these
nations that remain among you and if you intermarry with them and
associate with them, then you may be sure that the LORD your God will
no longer drive out these nations before you. Instead, they will become
snares and traps for you, whips on your backs and thorns in your eyes,
until you perish from this good land, which the LORD your God has
given you."

Instead of heeding Joshua's warning, the people have let a great wave
of wickedness wash over them. Its steady undertow pulls them further
and further from God.

Because of their failure to follow him, thousands of Israelites have been routed by just one man, whose name is Sisera. He is a ruthless mercenary who answers only to Jabin, the king of Canaan, who rules in Hazor, to the north. Because of his people's unfaithfulness, God has allowed Sisera to harass and oppress them for twenty years. By now, so much wickedness is abroad in the land that the roads are mostly empty. No one dares travel them, and the people are impoverished.

But God has not completely turned his face away. Instead, his ear is inclined toward them as he listens for the laments of his people, hoping they will cry out to him so he can restore their fortunes once more. It is for this very purpose that he has raised up Deborah to lead them, a woman bolder than any man.

One day God speaks to her. Quickly she sends word to Barak, the son of Abinoam from Kedish in the north. "The LORD, the God of Israel, commands you," she says. "'Go, take with you ten thousand men of Naphtali and Zebulun and lead them up to Mount Tabor. I will lead Sisera, the commander of Jabin's army, with his chariots and his troops to the Kishon River and give him into your hands.'"

But this is a fearful errand, and Barak knows he is no Moses. Nor is he a Joshua. He is only a man who wants to live and let live, to enjoy a little peace. But there is no peace.

Attempting to bridge the gap between what he fears and what God is asking, he sends word to Deborah: "If you go with me, I will go; but if you don't go with me, I won't go." Using Deborah as his banner, he knows he can rally the troops and raise an army to follow him.

But Deborah is unimpressed with his response. "Very well," she says, "I will go with you. But because of the way you are going about this, the honor will not be yours, for the LORD will hand Sisera over to a woman."

So Deborah heads ninety miles north to Kedesh in order to join Barak. With her on his side, he is able to raise an army of ten thousand men. Heading south, they plan to lure Sisera into battle.

Meanwhile, a Kenite by the name of Heber,* who is encamped

---

* A man with divided loyalties, Heber was at peace with Jabin, Sisera's overlord. But he is also a descendant of Moses' brother-in-law, Hobab, who helped the Israelites find their way through the wilderness. See Numbers 10:29–32.

near Kedesh, lets slip to Sisera that Barak and his army have gone up to Mount Tabor. Seizing his chance to quash the rebellion, Sisera leads his army and nine hundred chariots straight into battle.

As always, he is supremely confident. He is certain his chariots will make him unbeatable. But wily Barak has led his troops up the mountain, where chariots cannot go. Still Sisera knows that the Israelites must sooner or later come down and face him.

Meanwhile, Deborah is encamped on the mountain along with Barak and his troops. She arms herself, not with the weapons of war, but with prayer to the God who loves her. Refusing to entertain thoughts of how a ruthless enemy might treat a woman captured in battle, her ear is tuned to God's voice. As soon as she hears it, she turns to Barak and says: "Go! This is the day the LORD has given Sisera into your hands. Has not the LORD gone ahead of you?"

With Deborah's thunder ringing in his ears, Barak and his men rush down the mountain to meet Sisera and his dreaded chariots. Tearing through sheets of rain that shroud the valley below, the Israelite troops see what Deborah has already seen—that God is fighting for them. The sudden rains have caused the River Kishon to overflow its banks, turning the field of battle into a mucky swamp. Suddenly Sisera's greatest strength—his nine hundred chariots—has become his greatest weakness. Mired in mud, he and his chariots are an easy target.

So Barak and his men descend on Sisera's army, slaughtering every man but one.

Sisera escapes his chariot and flees on foot. His sturdy legs carry him mile after mile. When he thinks he can run no more, he keeps on running. At last he spots a place of refuge in the storm. Ahead of him loom the tents of Heber the Kenite. Sisera knows that Heber and his people are at peace with Jabin and thus with him.

But as he draws near to Heber's tents, it is not the Kenite who greets him but his wife, Jael. Though Sisera's distress is evident, she hails him, not as the battle's obvious loser, but as a friend in need of help. "Come, my lord," she says. "Come into my tent. Don't be afraid." He hesitates for just one moment because it is scandalous for a man to enter a woman's tent. But then it dawns on him. He has found the perfect hiding place. No one will think to look for him there.

Tenderly, as though she is caring for one of her children, Jael covers him as he lies down on the floor of her tent. Then she pours him a drink of milk and tells him to rest.

"Stand in the doorway of the tent," he commands her. "If someone comes by and asks you, 'Is anyone here?' say 'No.'"

She nods her assent, but he misses the small curl in her lip and the glint in her eyes as she leaves. Sisera knows only too well what men are capable of. But he has no idea what a woman can do. So he falls fast asleep.

Jael is a clever and hearty soul who is used to women's work, like taking down tents and putting them up again. Now she bends to the task at hand, reaching for a hammer and a large tent peg. Without a wasted movement and no hesitation in her steps, she walks silently to Sisera's side. He is exhausted, curled up in a ball and sleeping soundly. With a silent prayer and a steady aim, Jael raises her arm and then drives the tent peg straight through his temple, pinning his head to the ground.

Then she waits. When Barak comes by in hot pursuit, Jael comes out to greet him. "Come," she says, "I will show you the man you're looking for." So Barak follows her only to find that his enemy has already been slain. Wicked Sisera, the mighty general, has suffered the most shameful death a warrior can endure. He has perished by a woman's hand.

From that day forward the hand of the Israelites grows stronger and stronger, and Jabin, the Canaanite king, grows weaker and weaker until at last he is destroyed.

On the very day Sisera perishes, Deborah and Barak sing this song:

"Most blessed of women be Jael,
    the wife of Heber the Kenite,
    most blessed of tent-dwelling women....
Her hand reached for the tent peg,
    her right hand for the workman's hammer.
She struck Sisera, she crushed his head,
    she shattered and pierced his temple.
At her feet he sank,
    he fell; there he lay.
At her feet he sank, he fell;
    where he sank, there he fell—dead....
So may all your enemies perish, LORD!

But may all who love you be like the sun
when it rises in its strength."

Thus ends the story of how Deborah arose, a mother in Israel, and how Jael, a tent-dwelling woman, shamed the enemy and delivered the people God loved.

After that the land of Israel enjoyed peace for forty years.

## THE TIMES

Their story probably took place around 1209 BC.
Deborah ruled Israel between 1209–1169 BC.
*Deborah and Jael's story is told in Judges 4–5.*

Prophecy was common in the ancient Near East. In many pagan kingdoms, prophets were installed to affirm the policies of the reigning king. By contrast, true prophets in Israel were called by God and accountable only to him. Often, their messages were delivered in opposition to Israel's unfaithful rulers.

Among the patriarchal society of Israel, women rarely held leadership positions. One exception was in the area of prophecy, in which women as well as men could be prophets. In addition to being a prophetess, Deborah was considered a judge or leader in Israel before the Israelites had kings. Unlike modern judges, the leaders referred to in the book of Judges were hero-deliverers whom God raised up in order to rescue his people whenever they repented of their sins and cried out to him for help.

By choosing two women to rescue his people, one of whom was a foreigner, God was shaming his enemies and showcasing his own great strength, as though tying one hand behind his back to defeat them.

Of the two women in the story, Jael would have shocked her contemporaries the most. Throughout her story, she always took the initiative. Even though her husband was at peace with Jabin and therefore with Sisera, she appears to have acted independently, thus breaking their treaty. It would also have been considered highly improper for her to greet Sisera and invite him into her tent. In addition, hospitality in the ancient Near East was considered a sacred obligation, so sacred that the host was expected to protect his guests at the cost of his life if necessary. Yet Jael reverses the usual formula by killing the man who has taken refuge in her tent. Even in the final scene, she takes the initiative by stepping outside her tent to meet Barak when he comes looking for Sisera.

Just as Deborah had prophesied, the glory for the victory went not to Barak but to a woman. Actually, it went to two women. To Deborah who began the war and to Jael who finished it.

## THE TAKEAWAY

1. In the Old Testament, God often judged people by allowing them to suffer the natural consequences of their failure to trust and obey him. How does that dynamic play out in today's world, in the lives of individuals and nations?

2. Through Deborah, God promised he would go ahead of his people and fight for them. How has God fought on your behalf?

3. Throughout the Old Testament and especially in the book of Judges, we see a clear pattern emerge. God's people cry out for help. He rescues them. They fall away and become oppressed. They cry out for help. He rescues them. What does this cycle tell us about God? About human nature? About what to do when you feel oppressed?

4. When was the last time God asked you to do something you were afraid to do? How did you respond? What were the results?

# CHAPTER 7

# A Wicked Girlfriend

## THE STORY OF DELILAH

*For at the window of my house I looked through my casement,
and beheld among the simple ones, I discerned among the
youths, a young man void of understanding, passing through
the street near her corner; and he went the way to her house,
in the twilight, in the evening, in the black and dark night....
So she caught him, and kissed him, and with an impudent
face said unto him.... Come, let us take our fill of love until the
morning: let us solace ourselves with loves.... He goeth after
her straightway, as an ox goeth to the slaughter, or as a fool
to the correction of the stocks ... for she hath cast down many
wounded: yea, many strong men have been slain by her.*

Proverbs 7:6 – 9, 13, 18, 22, 26

$\mathcal{S}$he sleeps in the crook of his arm, her head nestled against his massive chest. At times his snoring is so loud, she thinks it will lift the roof of her house. Then he grunts and moans, turning his head in a moment of fitfulness. Despite the occasional nightmare, he never wakes until the first ray of light shines beneath her door. He slumbers so soundly that Delilah is sure he could sleep through the end of the world.

Before they go to bed, Samson tells her stories. Most of them are about his favorite subject—himself as a child, himself as a young man, himself as a leader in Israel. He says an angel foretold his birth and that he has always been consecrated to God. He regales her with tales of how he tore a lion apart with his bare hands and slew a thousand of his enemies with only the jawbone of a donkey. Oh, how he hates those donkeys, the Philistines.

Nothing will restrain his tongue when it comes to declaiming their worthlessness. He talks of setting their fields on fire to destroy their grain crops and of spreading terror wherever he goes. He considers it payback for how they've treated him and his people, the Israelites.

Quick to indulge his urge for power as well as pleasure, he is confident that nothing can stop him because he is the Lord's anointed—the hero of the story God is telling. A one-man army, he has led his people now for twenty years.

Not long ago a group of men gathered inside the gates of Gaza. They were planning to murder him as soon as he departed. (He does not tell Delilah he was spending the night with a prostitute.) But as soon as he saw them, he took hold of the heavy wooden gates, together with the two posts, and tore them loose, bar and all. Then he lifted them up and threw them away, leaving the city of Gaza defenseless.

A great roar escapes his mouth as he recalls the details. His laughter is so loud Delilah jumps when she hears it, and that makes him laugh all the more.

But she already knows of his exploits. His power is what makes him so attractive — at least to Delilah. She likes the hardness of his muscles, the girth of his arms as they enfold her. He is invincible, she thinks, and often tells him so.

Samson basks in her admiration, and it only takes a little flattery to keep him talking. She snuggles closer as he speaks about Abraham and Sarah and how God promised this land to his people. She knows of Moses and how Miriam led the victory dance at the edge of the Red Sea. And she can almost see Deborah and Barak celebrating their victory over Sisera.

But if their God has done such marvels, she wonders why Israel seems so weak. Samson has told her that two of the twelve tribes have been fighting against each other and that the rest are harassed by outside enemies. But Samson only shrugs when she asks why they are weak. He doesn't bother to tell her about the people's unfaithfulness or about how keeping God's commands is tied to Israel's prosperity. Nor does he speak about the time when some of his own people betrayed him to the Philistines. What toadies they are! Always bowing and scraping in front of their foreign overlords.

Samson is the biggest man Delilah has ever seen, but she knows he is not large enough to have performed so many wonders by himself. Some say that when the Spirit falls on him, he is strong enough to lift two mountains and hold them in his hands. She almost believes the tales they tell. For the moment, she is content to let the source of his strength remain a mystery. It is enough to bask in his power.

One day when Samson is away, Philistine rulers approach her. A fierce, seafaring people who have settled on the coast, they are used to being the ones who harass and oppress. If it were not for this one man, they could do as they please. But he is like a traveling avalanche, a man who wreaks havoc wherever he goes.

Though power has always been Delilah's favorite aphrodisiac, now they tempt her with something even more seductive — cold hard cash. Enough to keep her secure for the rest of her life.

"You are beautiful," they say, telling her what she already knows. "And Samson is under your thumb." She knows that too.

Then they offer her a bribe. "If you can lure him into telling you the secret of his power so that we are able to subdue him, we will each give you eleven hundred shekels of silver." It is an astonishing amount, an offer that reveals how desperate these men are.

It does not take long for Delilah to switch sides, and so she plays a game with Samson, asking him to reveal the secret of his great strength so he can be tied and subdued.

Samson loves this about her, that she is both beautiful and playful, and so he humors her, saying, "If anyone ties me with seven fresh thongs that have not been dried, I'll become as weak as any other man."

So the Philistines supply her with seven fresh thongs with which to bind him. While his enemies are hidden in the room, she exclaims, "Samson, the Philistines are upon you!" But he simply snaps the thongs as though they are tiny strings, and the secret of his great strength remains a mystery.

"You've made a fool of me," she scolds. "Come now, tell me the truth about how you can be tied." Then she caresses him as though to say she has already forgiven him.

Still toying with her, he replies, "If anyone ties me securely with new ropes that have never been used, I'll become as weak as any other man."

Delilah falls for the lie and ties him up again, crying, "Samson, the Philistines are upon you!" But as before, Samson merely snaps the ropes as though they are threads, and his enemies quickly flee.

This time she sulks and swats at him. When he grabs her wrist to draw her close, she demands the truth.

Sighing, as though to signal she has finally won the game, he tells her: "If you weave the seven braids of my head into the fabric on the loom and tighten it with the pin, I'll become as weak as any other man."

One day, while he lies snoring, Delilah weaves his long hair into the fabric on the loom* just as he has instructed.

In yet another comedic moment, Delilah cries out, telling Samson he is caught in the Philistine snare. But he simply sits up, yanking his hair from the loom.

Now she is angry. "How can you say, 'I love you,'" she accuses, "when you won't confide in me? This is the third time you have made a fool of me and haven't told me the secret of your great strength!"

---

* Possibly a horizontal loom fastened to the floor.

Delilah's accusations are a never-ending siege that finally wears him down.

One day he tells her the truth. "No razor has ever been used on my head," he says, "because I have been a Nazirite* dedicated to God from my mother's womb. If my head were shaved, my strength would leave me, and I would become as weak as any other man."

Sensing she has finally heard the truth, Delilah sends word to the Philistine rulers. This time they come loaded with a trove of silver.†

As Samson sleeps with his head on her lap, a man shaves off his seven braids. This time when Delilah wakes him, exclaiming, "Samson, the Philistines are upon you!" he rouses himself, intending to break free just as he has always done. It takes a few moments for him to realize that he has become as weak as other men because God has left him.

Delilah cups her hands over her ears to drown out his screams as the Philistines gouge out his eyes.‡ Then they drag him off to Gaza. Later she hears the story of how they humiliate him in prison, forcing him to grind out grain as though he is a woman.

In a few months, she hears they are holding a great festival. The Philistines are lovers of Dagon, the god of grain. Now the man who tried to destroy their grain by setting their fields on fire is completely in their power. Thousands are gathered along with their rulers in Dagon's temple, eager for a glimpse of the strong man who is called out for their amusement. As soon as they see him, they praise Dagon, saying,

"Our god has delivered our enemy
    into our hands,
the one who laid waste our land
    and multiplied our slain."

But the Philistines are in for a nasty surprise. For Samson's God has entered the house, and Dagon is going down. Blind and shackled though he is, Samson's hair has grown long again, and he can feel his strength returning. Confident that God is with him, he is plotting his revenge.

---

* Numbers 6:1–8 indicates that someone under a Nazirite vow was to abstain from three things: (1) any kind of intoxicating drink, including eating grapes or raisins; (2) cutting his hair; and (3) coming into contact with a dead body, either human or animal.

† Approximately 140 pounds of silver.

‡ A common practice in the ancient Near East, especially when dealing with particularly dangerous captives.

"Put me," he asks his guard, "where I can feel the pillars that support the temple, so that I may lean against them." To convince the guard, he slumps a little, as though he is only a blind man worn out from too much work. But once in position, he stretches out his arms, placing each hand against a pillar and praying: "O Sovereign LORD, remember me. Please God, strengthen me just once more, and let me with one blow get revenge on the Philistines for my two eyes.... Let me die with the Philistines."

Then Samson pushes with all his might, and Dagon's temple comes crashing down, crushing everyone beneath it and killing three thousand men and women who are standing on the roof.

As the news spreads throughout the region, Delilah can hear the wailing. The Philistines are grieving because of the shame that has come to their god and for the loss of so many people.

But hardly anyone mourns for Samson. Chosen by God for a singular role—to begin the liberation of his people—he managed to fulfill it, not by becoming wise and good, but by completing a final act of self-destructive violence. In death, Samson killed more of Israel's enemies than he had killed during his lifetime. Strong on the outside but weak on the inside, he ruled Israel for twenty years.

As for Delilah? She misses Samson just a little, but not too much. Instead of lament, her heart is filled with visions of the good life she has managed to secure for herself. No longer dependent on a man to meet her needs, she can do exactly as she pleases. Her future feels secure. Some would call her heartless, gullible, or stupid. But she merely calls herself lucky—free and rich beyond her dreams.

## THE TIMES

Her story probably takes place about 1055 BC.
*Delilah's story is drawn from Judges 13–16.*

Unlike the book of Joshua, which highlights a glorious period of conquest in Israel's history, the book of Judges tells of a time of terrible decline, in which "everyone did as they saw fit" (21:25). Samson was a primary example of this tendency, a man whose prodigious strength could not compensate for his moral weakness.

As they settled in Canaan, many of the Israelites began to practice idolatry, worshiping pagan deities like Baal (the god of storms and fertility) and Ashtoreth (the goddess of war and fertility). Repeating the pattern of Exodus, in which the journey from Egypt to Canaan should have been marked by days rather than years, the conquest and consolidation of Israel's power in the Promised Land took between three to four hundred years, showcasing the consequences of the Israelites' failure to trust God enough to obey him.

During the roughly two-hundred-year period described in the book of Judges, there is no clear evidence that any of the judges represented all the tribes of Israel. Sometimes judges arose concurrently in opposition to localized oppression.

Samson and Delilah lived in a period in which the Philistines ruled over southwestern Palestine. A seafaring people who had emigrated from the Aegean, they settled along the coast of Israel and then began to move eastward. The word *Palestine* is derived from their name.

Though the Israelites had not yet grasped Iron Age technology, the Philistines probably knew how to smelt and forge metal products, including those made out of iron. This knowledge gave them a strong military edge, helping them advance against people who were already settled in Canaan. Though the Philistines had their own distinct culture, including language, dress, weapons, and pottery, they quickly adopted Canaanite religious practices, including the worship of the god Dagon.

Though the text does not identify Delilah's ethnicity, she may have been a Philistine.

# THE TAKEAWAY

1. Delilah is one of the few female characters in the Bible whose character seems entirely negative. If you were to think of her as a more multifaceted character, what fears or insecurities do you imagine might have been behind her choices and behaviors?

2. In the story, Delilah appears to function primarily as a snare to a man who was chosen by God to lead his people. What kind of snares do you face in your efforts to live for God?

3. As a rule, women possessed little power in the ancient world in which Delilah's story unfolds. As often happens in such circumstances, Delilah used manipulation to get her way. How have you been tempted to use manipulation when you've felt powerless?

4. Why do you think God worked through an unsavory character like Samson? What does this story reveal about God and about his plans?

# CHAPTER 8

# Wicked Times

## THE STORY OF NAOMI AND RUTH

### How Two Desperate Women Find a
### Home and a Future Full of Hope

*Give, and it shall be given unto you; good measure, pressed
down, and shaken together, and running over, shall men give
into your bosom. For with the same measure that ye mete
withal it shall be measured to you again.*

Luke 6:38

$\mathcal{A}$t least six hundred years have passed since Tamar disguised herself as a harlot and tricked her father-in-law into sleeping with her. Their one-night stand produced twin boys, the eldest of whom was Perez. It was through him that God preserved the tribe of Judah.

Now, in the time of the judges, when there is no king and chaos rules, lives a man named Elimelek, who is descended from Perez. He dwells in a village called Bethlehem, which means "house of bread," though there is hardly any bread to be found in all the land of Judah.

To preserve his family, Elimelek takes his wife, Naomi, and his two sons, Mahlon and Kilion, and heads east toward the rich highlands of Moab on the other side of the Dead Sea. In Moab* there are rivers and rainfall and food enough for everyone. He leaves reluctantly, hoping this will be the briefest of sojourns. But neither he nor his sons will ever see Bethlehem again.

Though Naomi has little to eat, she is grateful that God has filled her house with the noisy banter of a husband and two sons. She knows she will be content as long as her family stays together.

But while they are in Moab, tragedy strikes. Elimelek falls ill and then dies. His passing is so swift and the pain of his loss is so sharp that Naomi wonders how she will survive it.

As for her sons Mahlon and Kilion, they are now grown men with Moabite wives, named Orpah and Ruth, both of whom Naomi loves. In the midst of her grief, she makes a point of thanking God that even though she is a widow, she is not destitute. She has two loving sons and their wives to care for her.

She does not know that tragedy will soon strike again.

In quick succession both of Naomi's sons die. Now there is not merely one widow who needs looking after but three, and all of them

---

* Genesis 19:37 indicates that the Moabites were descended from Moab, who was the product of an incestuous relationship between Abraham's nephew Lot and Lot's eldest daughter.

are facing ruin. To have no husband is a tragedy. But to be without children is a curse. With the loss of her husband and sons, Naomi is wild with grief and fear. A foreigner in Moab, she has no one to care for her. Surely God must be displeased with her to have taken her husband and both of her sons.

Before long, word reaches her that the land of Judah has been blessed with rain and abundant crops. The drought is finally over. Despite the fact that the road from Moab to Bethlehem is thick with thieves, Naomi decides to risk the journey. Her daughters-in-law, Orpah and Ruth, insist on coming with her. God willing, the three women will arrive in time for the April harvest.

As much as she loves them, Naomi has misgivings. Before the three have journeyed far, she turns to her daughters-in-law, and says, "Go back, each of you, to your mother's home. May the LORD show kindness to you, as you have shown to your dead husbands and to me. May the LORD grant that each of you will find rest in the home of another husband."

As she kisses them in final farewell, the two young women weep and cling to her. They cannot bring themselves to let her face the dangers of the road alone.

But Naomi will not give up. "Return home, my daughters. Why would you come with me? Am I going to have any more sons, who could become your husbands? Return home, my daughters; I am too old to have another husband. Even if I thought there was still hope for me — even if I had a husband tonight and then gave birth to sons — would you wait until they grew up? Would you remain unmarried for them? No, my daughters. It is more bitter for me than for you, because the LORD's hand has turned against me!"[23]

Naomi believes this. That God hates her.

But Orpah loves her. Even so, she agrees with the wisdom of Naomi's argument. Why would anyone in the land of Judah want to marry an impoverished Moabite widow? Tearfully, wishing the world was different than it is, she kisses her mother-in-law good-bye and then returns to Moab. But Ruth refuses to leave.

Once again Naomi presses her. "Ruth," she says. "Your sister-in-law is going back to her people and her gods. Go back with her."

But the young woman will not listen. "Don't urge me to leave you or to turn back from you. Where you go I will go, and where you stay I will stay. Your people will be my people and your God my God.* Where you die I will die, and there I will be buried. May the LORD deal with me, be it ever so severely, if even death separates you and me."

Beautiful, amazing Ruth! Naomi is relieved that her daughter-in-law has finally won their argument.

After several days, the two arrive safely in Bethlehem, an event that stirs considerable excitement. "Can this be Naomi?" her neighbors exclaim, amazed that ten years have passed since she and her family moved to Moab.

"Don't call me Naomi," she replies. "Call me Mara, because the Almighty has made my life very bitter. I went away full, but the LORD has brought me back empty. Why call me Naomi?† The LORD has afflicted me; the Almighty has brought misfortune upon me." Then she speaks of her great anguish, of the emptiness she feels at losing her husband and sons.

Naomi has become what each of the women fears most, a widow with no obvious means of support.

Though Ruth still grieves the loss of her husband, it eases her pain to think about taking care of Naomi. For all her complaints, her mother-in-law is not hard to love. With Naomi's blessing, she heads out to the fields to glean whatever the harvesters have missed. More than mere custom, the practice is enshrined in law — every landowner must refrain from reaping the edges of his field, thereby allowing the poor to gather whatever is left behind. If she's lucky, Ruth will harvest enough grain to keep herself and Naomi alive. But the work is rough and dangerous, especially for a young foreign woman without family members to avenge an insult.

Ruth begins working in a field that belongs to a man named Boaz. Midmorning, she notices him talking with his foreman and then heading her way. A tall man with grey, shoulder-length hair and a broad, welcoming smile, he greets her. "My daughter," he says, "listen to me.

---

* Most people in the ancient Near East worshiped gods whom they believed operated only among their own people in a certain geographical region. Leaving Moab, Ruth must also leave behind the gods of Moab.

† *Naomi* means "pleasant." *Mara* means "bitter."

Don't go and glean in another field and don't go away from here. Stay here with my servant girls. Watch the field where the men are harvesting, and follow along after the girls. I have told the men not to lay a hand on you. And whenever you are thirsty, go and get a drink from the water jars the men have filled."

Surprised by his kindness, Ruth bows and then exclaims, "Why have I found such favor in your eyes that you notice me—a foreigner?"

"I've been told all about what you have done for your mother-in-law since the death of your husband," he says, "how you left your father and mother and your homeland and came to live with a people you did not know before. May the LORD repay you for what you have done. May you be richly rewarded by the LORD, the God of Israel, under whose wings you have come to take refuge."

His words feel like a benediction.

Later that day, Boaz offers Ruth a generous portion of bread and roasted grain to eat. Then he instructs his men: "Even if she gathers among the sheaves, don't embarrass her. Rather, pull out some stalks for her from the bundles and leave them for her to pick up, and don't rebuke her."

Ruth works hard until evening. After threshing the barley, she measures the day's haul—two thirds of a bushel, enough to feed Naomi and herself for several weeks! As she makes her way home, she notices a bird alighting on its nest. Thinking of the chicks that shelter beneath its wings, she thanks God that she has found her own place under his all-sheltering wings.

When Ruth arrives home, Naomi is astonished. She can't believe how much grain Ruth has harvested in a single day. "Whose field did you glean in? Blessed be the man who took notice of you!"

When Naomi learns that the field is Boaz's, she exclaims, "That man is our close relative; he is one of our guardian-redeemers."

As April passes into May, Ruth continues to work in Boaz's field. One day, her mother-in-law hatches a plan. "My daughter," Naomi says, "shouldn't I try to find a home for you, where you will be well provided for? Tonight Boaz will be winnowing barley on the threshing floor. This is what you must do. Perfume yourself and wear your best clothes and then go down to the threshing floor. But don't let him see you until he's finished eating and drinking. Note the place where he lies down. Afterward, go to him, uncover his feet, and lie down. He will tell you what to do."

So Ruth does exactly as Naomi tells her. She watches where Boaz lies down at the far end of the grain pile. He and his men will spend the night on the threshing floor in order to protect the harvest. Once all is quiet, Ruth lies down beside Boaz, uncovering his feet.*

She trembles as she does so, wondering how Boaz will react when he wakes up. Then she drifts into sleep. And as she dreams, she sees an enormous eagle, hovering above her, and she hears him singing these words: *If you make the Most High your dwelling, he will cover you with his feathers, and under his wings you will find refuge.*

At midnight Boaz awakens, startled to discover a woman lying at his feet. "Who's there?" he demands.

"I am your servant Ruth," she says. "Spread the corner of your garment† over me, since you are a guardian-redeemer of our family."

Realizing that she is proposing marriage, Boaz replies: "The LORD bless you, my daughter. This kindness is greater than that which you showed earlier: You have not run after the younger men, whether rich or poor. And now, my daughter, don't be afraid. I will do for you all you ask. Although it is true that I am a guardian-redeemer of our family, there is a another who is more closely related than I. Stay here for the night, and in the morning if he wants to do his duty as your guardian-redeemer, good; let him redeem you. But if he is not willing, as surely as the LORD lives I will do it."

Ruth lies at his feet until morning but departs before sunrise so no one will notice her presence. Before she goes, Boaz pours six measures of barley into her shawl.

Then he heads straight into town and waits at the gate until the man who is Naomi's close relative passes by. When he finds him, he says, "Naomi, who has come back from Moab, is selling the piece of land that belonged to our relative Elimelek. I thought I should bring the matter

---

* After the work was done, the threshers would feast together and then bed down for the night to protect the grain. Though the threshing floor at night was a male stronghold, it was sometimes visited by prostitutes.

† *kānāp* is translated as "corner of your garment." It can also be translated as "wings." Covering someone with the corner of your garment symbolizes marriage and is a custom still practiced in parts of the Middle East.

to your attention and suggest that you buy it in the presence of these seated here and in the presence of the elders of my people. If you will redeem it, do so. But if you will not, tell me, so I will know. For no one has the right to do it except you, and I am next in line."

"I will redeem it," the man replies, glad for the chance to add land to his holdings.

But there is a catch, which Boaz now reveals. "On the day you buy the land from Naomi and from Ruth the Moabitess, you acquire the dead man's widow, in order to maintain the name of the dead with his property."

This is too much for the man, who quickly retracts his offer. He's in no position to acquire a new wife whose future offspring will take the name of Ruth's first husband and then inherit the land.

After Boaz has cleverly cleared the path for himself, he proclaims his love for Ruth in the presence of all the people. So Ruth becomes his wife, and she gives birth to a son. His name is Obed, and he will become the father of Jesse, who will become the father of David, who will become Israel's greatest king.

As everyone knows, it is from David's line that the Savior will be born.

Because of two desperate women and the God who cared for them, the world would one day come to know another Guardian-Redeemer. He would be the one to deliver his people, wiping out their debts and giving them a future filled with hope.

## THE TIMES

*Their story takes place sometime between 1400 and 1050 BC.*
*Naomi and Ruth's story is told in the book of Ruth.*

A widow without sons to support her after her husband's death might become so destitute that she would have to sell herself into slavery or prostitution to survive. For instance, though God commanded his people to care for widows, many of the Mosaic laws were ignored during the era of the judges. Though the law (Leviticus 19:9–10; 23:22; Deuteronomy 24:19–21) instructed landowners to leave some produce in their fields for the poor to glean, many landowners simply ignored this provision.

In addition to gleaning and levirate marriage, a widow could appeal to a guardian-redeemer, or *go'el*, to act on her behalf. In such cases, the closest male relative was expected to rescue or deliver her (or other impoverished family members) by paying off debts or buying back properties that had been sold, because without land people could barely survive.

The New Testament portrays Jesus as our great Guardian-Redeemer, the one who through his self-sacrifice pays off every debt our sins have incurred, delivering us from evil and setting us free.

# THE TAKEAWAY

1. Throughout Scripture, God sometimes chooses to rename people to indicate a greater purpose for their lives, e.g., "Abram" becomes "Abraham," "Sarai" becomes "Sarah," and "Simon" becomes "Cephas." In this case, it is not God but Naomi who renames herself: "'Don't call me Naomi,' she told them. 'Call me Mara, because the Almighty has made my life very bitter. I went away full, but the LORD has brought me back empty. Why call me Naomi?'" What does this reveal about her state of mind? How would you rename yourself based on your own circumstances?

2. Naomi mistakenly thinks her suffering is a punishment from God. Have you ever felt that your hardships were evidence that God was displeased with you? Looking back, do you see it any differently now? Why or why not? How has that affected the way you've experienced periods of difficulty?

3. When Boaz first meets Ruth, he expresses the wish that God will repay her for her faith and kindness, never suspecting that he will become the answer to his prayer. Have you ever become the answer to a prayer that you or others have prayed? What were the circumstances?

4. The story of Naomi and Ruth is marked by a series of blessings. First Ruth blesses Naomi by staying with her. Then Naomi blesses Ruth by helping her find a husband. Boaz subsequently blesses Ruth with a home, and God blesses them both with a child. Afterward, the women of Bethlehem tell Naomi that she is blessed with a daughter-in-law who is worth more than seven sons. Think back over the last two or three days. In what ways would you say that God has both blessed you and made you a blessing to others?

# CHAPTER 9

# A Wicked Predicament

## THE STORY OF HANNAH AND PENINNAH

*My heart rejoiceth in the Lord, mine horn is exalted in the Lord: my mouth is enlarged over mine enemies; because I rejoice in thy salvation...*

*The Lord maketh poor, and maketh rich: he bringeth low, and lifteth up.*

1 Samuel 2:1, 7

$\mathcal{A}$ few years after Samson crushed the Philistines, a fat priest by the name of Eli is presiding as a judge in Shiloh. The last bad apple in the bowl, he is so heavy that the belt encircling his robe disappears into the quicksand of his flesh, and children speculate about how God might be able to create another human being out of his excess.

Whenever he is not officiating as high priest, Eli rests in his favorite chair, the one specially crafted to hold his girth. He watches at the doorpost of the tabernacle as men and women pass in and out.

Shiloh is the religious capital of the new nation, the place where Joshua first divided the land and then apportioned it by lottery to the twelve tribes of Israel. The sacred center of the universe, it is the place where the golden ark has come to rest, sheltered inside the Tent of Meeting. Each year thousands of pilgrims go up to Shiloh to celebrate the feasts.

One of these is a woman by the name of Peninnah. Though not great on the scale of wickedness, she has a nasty habit of using her tongue to fling countless tiny arrows at her enemies. With a large mouth and a nose that is always looking down on someone, she is the lesser favorite of Elkanah's two wives. Unlike her rival, Hannah, she is the mother of several children.

Every year it is the same. Elkanah and his two wives, along with their children, go up to Shiloh to worship the Lord and present their sacrifices. Along the way, Peninnah keeps pointing out the obvious. How sad that Hannah cannot have children. How fortunate for Elkanah that he has taken a second wife to perform the duty his first cannot. She thanks God for all the sons he has blessed her with so that she can make up for Hannah's lack. Truly God alone knows every heart—whom to bless and whom to curse. Blessed be the God of Israel.

As always, Peninnah's cruelty has found its mark in Hannah's heart, provoking her to tears. Each year the old wound opens up again as Peninnah's arrows thrust deeper.

Elkanah does his best to shush his disagreeable wife. Once he and Hannah are alone, he caresses her as she leans against his chest, trying to soothe her by asking, "Why are you weeping? Why don't you eat? Why are you downhearted? Don't I mean more to you than ten sons?"

How can Hannah tell her husband the truth—that though he is the best of men, he cannot heal the heartbreak that comes from not being able to bear a son?

The next day, Elkanah presents his offerings to God, and he and his family feast together as is the custom, partaking of their portion of the sacrifices. Afterward, Hannah makes her way to the sanctuary alone. There she enters the presence of the Holy One, who is the only one to whom she can pour out her heart's discontent. With tears spilling down her cheeks, and her lips moving inaudibly in prayer,* she makes a vow: "LORD Almighty, if you will only look on your servant's misery and remember me, and not forget your servant but give her a son, then I will give him to the LORD for all the days of his life, and no razor will ever be used on his head."

As Hannah is pouring out her heart to God, the old priest Eli is watching from the shadows. When he sees her moving her lips without making a sound, he scolds her: "How long are you going to stay drunk? Put away your wine."†

"Not so, my lord," she says. "I am a woman who is deeply troubled. I have not been drinking wine or beer; I was pouring out my soul to the LORD. Do not take your servant for a wicked woman; I have been praying out of my great anguish and grief."

"Go in peace," he tells her, "and may the God of Israel grant you what you have asked of him."

Afterward, Elkanah notices that Hannah's sadness has lifted. Once they arrive home, the two make love, and this time God blesses them with a son. Hannah names him Samuel, which sounds like the Hebrew word for "heard of God." Pledging him to the Lord forever, she plans to bring her boy to Shiloh once he is weaned, in about three years' time.

When the day arrives, she and Elkanah take their little son up to the house of the Lord. While Peninnah and her children look on, Hannah

---

* Prayers were usually prayed out loud.

† Jesus' disciples were also accused of drunkenness when they were filled with the Holy Spirit on Pentecost. See Acts 2:1–13.

turns to Eli and declares, "Pardon me, my lord. As surely as you live, I am the woman who stood here beside you praying to the LORD. I prayed for this child, and the LORD has granted me what I asked of him. So now I give him to the LORD. For his whole life he will be given over to the LORD."

Though it has been a long time since Eli has stood this close to a miracle, he merely nods his head in assent and takes the boy in hand. As Hannah kisses her only child good-bye, a solitary tear runs down her cheek. Before she leaves, she sings this prayer,

> "My heart rejoices in the LORD;
>   in the LORD my horn* is lifted high.
> My mouth boasts over my enemies,
>   for I delight in your deliverance.
> There is no one holy like the LORD;
>   there is no one besides you;
>   there is no Rock like our God.
> Do not keep talking so proudly
>   or let your mouth speak such arrogance,
> for the LORD is a God who knows,
>   and by him deeds are weighed.
> The bows of the warriors are broken,
>   but those who stumbled are armed with strength.
> Those who were full hire themselves out for food,
>   but those who were hungry hunger no more.
> She who was barren has borne seven† children,
>   but she who has had many sons pines away.
> The LORD brings death and makes alive;
>   he brings down to the grave and raises up.
> The LORD sends poverty and wealth;
>   he humbles and he exalts.
> He raises the poor from the dust
>   and lifts the needy from the ash heap;
> he seats them with princes
>   and has them inherit a throne of honor.
> For the foundations of the earth are the LORD's;
>   on them he has set the world.

---

\* Animals often use their horns or antlers as weapons. Here Hannah invokes an image of strength and majesty, perhaps also suggesting prosperity and progeny.

† Even though Hannah will give birth to six children, the number "seven" symbolizes perfection. As such it invokes her satisfaction at all the ways God will bless her.

He will guard the feet of his saints,
　　but the wicked will be silenced in the place of darkness.
It is not by strength that one prevails;
　　those who oppose the LORD will be broken.
The Most High will thunder from heaven;
　　the LORD will judge the ends of the earth.
He will give strength to his king
　　and exalt the horn of his anointed."

Though Peninnah feigns indifference, she cannot help but note the words of Hannah's song, especially the ones that pertain to her. Like arrows they pierce her heart.

As for Hannah, she becomes the happy mother of two daughters and three more sons. Every year, she and her family make the journey north to Shiloh to celebrate the feasts. Each time, she is amazed to see how much her boy has grown.

Unlike Eli, who, along with his two wicked sons, will come to a very bad end, Samuel will grow up to become a great man of God. He will be the last of the judges, a prophet who will anoint Saul, Israel's first king, and David, Israel's greatest king.

While Peninnah and her children will soon be forgotten, Hannah's story will echo through the centuries until another young mother lifts up her voice to proclaim the greatness of God.* Like Samuel, the child growing inside Mary will be born in answer to prayer, but not just the prayer of a solitary woman. Instead, her child will be the answer to the prayers of all God's people as they cry out to him for a Deliverer. Like Samuel, Mary's little boy will be destined to cause the falling and rising of many in Israel.

## THE TIMES

Her story takes place about 1105 BC.
*Hannah's story can be found in 1 Samuel 1:1–2:11.*
*Echoes of her prayer can be heard in Luke 1:46–55.*

After Joshua led the Israelites on their initial conquest of Israel, he erected a tabernacle at Shiloh, about twenty miles north of Jerusalem. For more than three hundred years, Shiloh served as the religious center

---

\* See Mary's prayer, which is often called "The Magnificat," in Luke 1:46–55.

of the new nation, until it was destroyed by the Philistines in about 1050 BC. More than a century passed until Israel once again had a central religious site. This time it was located in Jerusalem, in Solomon's temple, which was built around 966–959 BC.

In the early history of Israel, the practice of polygamy was generally reserved for wealthy families. Rather than stemming from uncontrolled sexual desire, it was more commonly practiced to achieve two ends — to continue the family line and to produce a large enough family to handle the labor-intensive demands of farming and raising livestock. Because ancient peoples believed that fertility was under divine control, infertility was often viewed as a curse.

Like the peoples around them, the Israelites had a sacrificial system of worship. When we think of sacrificing something, we often think of giving something away. Ancient peoples would more likely have thought in terms of giving something *over*. To the ancient Israelites, sacrifice always involved transformation. Whenever something was sacrificed, it was transferred from the common realm to the realm of the sacred. When Hannah and Elkanah brought their sacrifices to God at Shiloh, they were giving him gifts he had already given to them — animals, grain, and wine. Through such sacrifices, they were seeking to deepen their relationship with God.*

---

* For a more complete explanation of sacrifice at this time, see William K. Gilders, "Sacrifice in Ancient Israel," *Teaching the Bible: an e-newsletter for public school teachers by Society of Biblical Literature* (accessed May 2010), http://www.sbl-site.org/assets/pdfs/TBv2i5_Gilders2.pdf.

# THE TAKEAWAY

1. It is difficult to overestimate Hannah's pain at not being able to bear children, particularly given the culture in which she lived. How does her prayer (1 Samuel 1:10–16) point to a way out of despair?

2. Take a few moments to meditate on Hannah's song (1 Samuel 2:1–10). What words or phrases strike you? Why?

3. Hannah's song (pages 90–91) emphasizes a series of reversals—the hungry are filled, the barren woman gives birth, the poor are lifted up. What does she mean by saying, "It is not by strength that one prevails?" In what ways might your life or perspective change if you took this statement seriously?

4. Hannah prayed for a child, but God gave her so much more. The son she prayed for became Israel's last judge. As kingmaker, Samuel helped Israel make the transition from the chaotic period of the judges into the more ordered period of the monarchy, during which time the Israelites were finally able to subdue their enemies. What might this imply about the potential ramifications of our own prayers?

# CHAPTER 10

# A Wicked Snare

## THE STORY OF MICHAL

### How a Trophy Princess
### Falls Out of Love

*They also that seek after my life lay snares for me:
and they that seek my hurt speak mischievous
things, and imagine deceits all the day long.*

Psalm 38:12

*M*ichal's father is a head taller than most—strong, handsome, decisive. He hails from the warrior tribe of Benjamin. She cannot remember a time when her father was not king and she not a princess. She has heard how God instructed the prophet Samuel to anoint Saul as Israel's first king.

She knows, too, that the old prophet is not altogether happy about his choice. She has heard rumors that the two men have fallen out and that Samuel has told her father point blank that God is done with him. Saul is too much like the kings of other nations to meet with divine approval.

Despite Samuel's disapproval, Saul remains king. Though he is sturdier than most men, Michal senses something brittle within. He blows hot and cold, as though fast-moving clouds are casting sinister shadows across his soul. One moment he seems confident that his kingdom will last, while the next he is dejected and sour.

Though Michal is sensitive to prevailing winds, she is not interested in politics. Instead, a young warrior has turned her head. Handsome and lithe, they say he routed the Philistines by felling their champion, a god-awful man by the name of Goliath. While Saul's army cowered before this giant, only the shepherd boy David was willing to engage with him in single combat. Michal has heard the tale—how, refusing the protection of her father's armor, David prevailed with merely a sling and a stone.

Everything David does succeeds. Just days ago, she watched as women poured out of the city gates to greet David as he and Saul returned from battle. Hailing them, they sang,

"Saul has slain his thousands,
and David his tens of thousands."

Their singing makes her father furious. "They have credited David with tens of thousands.... What more can he get but the kingdom?" Saul complains.

She notes the way her father eyes David, as though he is no longer a favorite but a dangerous rival.

Her brother Jonathan is oblivious to Saul's jealousy. Instead of distancing himself from David, he draws him into his inner circle. The two men are so close that they have become like sandals on a single pair of feet. Jonathan is so taken by David that he makes him the gift of his tunic, sword, and belt. It is as much as saying that on the day David becomes king, he, the son of a king, will serve him.

Whenever Michal spots David in her father's court, she tries to catch his eye. Caring nothing for Saul's disapproval, she is unaware of how murderous his jealousy has become. Twice he has tried and failed to pin David to the wall with a spear. Now he can think of nothing but how to get rid of him.

One day, Saul learns that Michal is infatuated with David. The knowledge delights him, because she is just the snare he needs. So Saul instructs his servants to approach David with an offer: "Look, the king is pleased with you," they say. "He wants you for his son-in-law. All he asks for a bride price is that you take revenge on his enemies by bringing him a hundred Philistine foreskins."* Saul knows that such a task will likely lead to David's death, for the Philistines are fierce fighters.

Though Michal knows her father is merely using her as bait, she is thrilled to hear that David will attempt the challenge. Before long, David returns from his quest with not one hundred but two hundred Philistine foreskins!

So Michal and David marry, and even though they are living under the shadow of Saul's jealousy, they are happy for a time. At night, when they are alone, David sings to her:

"How beautiful you are, my darling!
  Oh, how beautiful!
  Your eyes behind your veil are doves.
Your lips are like a scarlet ribbon;
  your mouth is lovely.
Your breasts are like two fawns,
  like twin fawns of a gazelle

---

\* Mutilating enemies in this way was not uncommon. Unlike many of the surrounding peoples, the Philistines did not practice circumcision. By requesting a hundred foreskins, Saul can be sure that David has killed Philistines.

that browse among the lilies.
Until the day breaks
    and the shadows flee,
I will go to the mountain of myrrh
    and to the hill of incense.
You are altogether beautiful, my darling;
    there is no flaw in you."*

Michal loves the poetry that flows from David's soul. No wonder Saul once welcomed his songs with their strange power to drive away his demons and soothe his mind.

Her new husband is everything a princess could desire — passionate, strong, courageous, attentive, and handsome. Other women envy her, and that pleases Michal all the more.

One day word reaches her that her father is about to arrest David. Rushing to his side, she tells David, "If you don't run for your life tonight, tomorrow you'll be killed." In the darkness she lets her husband down through their open window and watches him disappear into the night.

Then she takes a large statue† and lays it on the bed, covering it with a garment and putting goat hair at the head. A crude ruse, it fools the slow-witted soldiers who come looking for David. "He is ill," Michal explains, "and cannot rise from his bed."

But Saul is furious when they return without him. "Bring him bed and all if you must!"

When the trick is revealed, his rage explodes, and he accuses Michal of betraying him. "Why did you deceive me like this and send my enemy away so he escaped?"

A lie slips quickly off her tongue: "David said to me, 'Let me get away. Why should I kill you?'"

In the months ahead, Michal yearns for her husband. She wonders how long it will be until he climbs up to her room and carries her away. From time to time she hears rumors of his exploits in desert regions to the south. Night after night she lies alone and lonely in their bed, feeling like the woman who sang:

---

* Though the poetry quoted here was not written by David but is part of the Song of Songs (4:1, 3, 5–7), David was a poet/musician and might well have composed a love song for Michal.

† Most scholars believe that Michal placed a household idol on the bed.

"All night long on my bed
   I looked for the one my heart loves;
   I looked for him but did not find him.
I will get up now and go about the city,
    through its streets and squares;
I will search for the one my heart loves.
   So I looked for him but did not find him."

Michal does not encounter David for many years. By now she has stopped looking for him, because she is married to Paltiel, the man she married after David's escape. She knows that Saul was merely spiting David by giving her to another man. It is just as Samuel said it would be when he warned the people what would happen when a king ruled over them. "You yourselves will become his slaves," he had said.

Now Michal feels the truth of this. Princess though she is, she knows she is merely a bird in a cage, a pawn for her father's power alliances. At least Paltiel loves her, and she has learned to love him too.

Though she doesn't know it, the last days of her father's reign are closing in. Before long he and three of her brothers, including Jonathan, will be killed and mutilated by Philistines, whose arrows overtake them during fierce fighting on Mount Gilboa.

After Saul's death, the twelve tribes of Israel split in two. Some declare their allegiance to Saul's son Ish-Bosheth while others follow David. Now that the king is dead, David demands Michal's return, and Ish-Bosheth agrees. Once more and without being consulted, Michal is torn from the husband she loves.

When Michal sees David again, she is amazed by his strength. Instead of the youth she married, she sees a man who has been hardened by war and who is determined to rule. The people flock to him, just as her father had feared they would. But despite his ascendancy, Michal cannot bring herself to love him. Too much time has passed. Too many questions remain unanswered. Why had David never returned for her? She could have fled with him into the desert away from her father's wrath. But he never came.

David wants her back, she thinks, but only to secure his power.

As for the young woman David married, she is gone forever. In her place stands a woman who has been thrown by fate into a life she does not want. Queen though she is, Michal feels bitter and forsaken.

Not long after she is returned to David, Michal's brother Ish-Bosheth is killed by two of his own henchmen. Now all the tribes of Israel pledge their loyalty to David. At last his kingdom is secure.

One day Michal walks to the window of David's palace and peers out. She listens as a large crowd winds its way up to Jerusalem with shouts and the clamor of trumpets. At the head of a great procession is the king himself. Instead of his royal robes, David wears the simple garments of a priest. He is dancing with all his might to the sound of songs and the music of harps, lyres, tambourines, and cymbals. Slowly the great golden ark of the covenant, the sacred place where God has decided to dwell, advances into the city. Yahweh has come to live among his people once again!

David leads the crowd in praise, singing,

"Look to the LORD and his strength;
    seek his face always.
Remember the wonders he has done,
    his miracles, and the judgments he pronounced....
Sing to the LORD, all the earth;
    proclaim his salvation day after day.
Declare his glory among the nations,
    his marvelous deeds among all peoples."

But Michal is not in the mood for singing, nor does she feel like rejoicing. She thinks only of her dead father and brothers. This moment should belong to them and not to David. This is their kingdom, not his, she thinks. She looks on as David leaps about, contorting his body in a wild dance of praise to God. When the dancing is over, he gives gifts of bread and cake to everyone present, and then he returns home to bless his household.

Michal, daughter of Saul, comes out to greet him, not with rejoicing as one might expect the queen to do, but with words designed to shame and scald: "How the king of Israel has distinguished himself today, going about half-naked in full view in the sight of the slave girls of his servants as any vulgar fellow would!"

But David merely answers: "It was before the LORD, who chose me rather than your father or anyone from his house when he appointed me ruler over the LORD's people Israel—I will celebrate before the LORD. I will become even more undignified than this, and I will be humiliated in my own eyes. But by these slave girls you spoke of, I will be held in honor."

And so it is that even to this day, David's memory is revered by all God's people.

As for Michal, her story ends in sadness. Living in David's palace she remained who she always was, a little bird trapped in a big cage, a pretty thing to please a man. Childless until the day of her death,* she had no one who could rise up and call her blessed.

## THE TIMES

She lived sometime between 1040–970 BC.
*Michal's story can be found in 1 Samuel 18:20–29;
19:11–17; 25:44; 2 Samuel 3:13–16; 6:16–23.*

Michal lived during a time of great transition, when Israel was leaving the chaotic period of the judges behind and entering the period of the monarchy. During the rule of the judges, Israel had great difficulty completing the conquest of Canaan and becoming a unified nation. But once the monarchy was established, Saul and David helped the Israelites defeat many of their surrounding enemies.

During this period many of the great powers in the region were in decline. The Hittites, Assyrians, Babylonians, and Egyptians had too many problems of their own to try to extend their influence into Canaan. Their weakness allowed David to extend the borders of his kingdom with great success. Only the Philistines who lived along the coast proved too hard to dislodge.

Though Samuel had anointed Saul as Israel's first king, it wasn't long before Saul proved himself unworthy by repeatedly disobeying the word of God as it was delivered by the prophet Samuel. Though Saul had rejected God, he reigned for forty-two years, until he committed

---

* The Bible doesn't indicate whether Michal was childless because of barrenness or because David refused to sleep with her. By refusing to have relations with her, he would have been ensuring there would be no rival claimants to his throne from the house of Saul. Those who heard her story would have likely seen Michal's childlessness as a curse.

suicide in order to avoid capture by the Philistines. David ruled for an additional forty years, and his son Solomon ruled for forty more years. After that, the nation was divided into the southern kingdom of Judah and the northern kingdom of Israel.

Unlike the rulers of other nations, Israel's king was called to be humble rather than proud. He was to read God's word and live by it. Rather than dominating the people, he was to consider himself one of them (Deuteronomy 17:19–20). The king was to be devoted to God, which Saul was not. Unfortunately, Michal suffered the consequences of her father's repeated disobedience and unfaithfulness.

## THE TAKEAWAY

1. Michal's story is a sad one. Born to royal privilege, she became a pawn of powers she could not control. It is hard not to sympathize with her even though her response to David injects a sour note into the story. What parts of Michal's story impact you most? In what ways, if any, do you relate to her?

2. Comment on Michal's seeming indifference when the ark of the covenant enters Jerusalem. What might this reveal about her spiritual condition?

3. Michal repeatedly finds herself at the mercy of forces she cannot control. What circumstances in your life have made you feel as though you have too little control? How have you responded? In what ways have you experienced or failed to experience God in such circumstances?

4. Michal experienced the loss of two husbands, a father, and four brothers. Her grief and bitterness over her losses made it difficult for her to move into a renewed relationship with David. How have your own hardships and losses affected your most important relationships?

# CHAPTER 11

# Wicked Smart

## THE STORY OF ABIGAIL

### How a Quick-Witted Woman
### Averts a Foolish Disaster

*The wise fear the L*ORD *and shun evil,*
*but a fool is hotheaded and yet feels secure.*
Proverbs 14:16 (NIV)

*T*hough his head is large, it seems like wasted space for a man who thinks only of the smallest things — like whether the latest delicacy has been properly prepared or his new robe is quite to his liking. Easily displeased, Nabal soothes himself with wine and pleasant food. Year after year, as his head grows emptier, his waist expands.

Despite his tendency toward complaint, he has to admit it has been a good year. Because his flocks have not been troubled by bandits, they have multiplied beyond expectation. He predicts the annual shearing will yield a record harvest — more than three tons of wool! Plus his profits have improved through shrewd negotiations with the shepherds who tend his flocks. This year their cut is even less than last year's. A thousand goats and three thousand sheep are far too many for one man to tend. Better to stay at home while his hired men spend their nights in the open, fending off predators.

Nabal knows other men despise him. But they are jealous, he thinks. The more he senses their disdain, the more he struts and brags. He is a rich man, and not afraid to show it. So what if people envy him? In addition to his wealth, he is married to a woman many men would covet. Abigail is a stunning creature, remarkably intelligent. The proof, he says, is that she married him. Chuckling over his frequently repeated jest, he fails to notice that his wife never smiles when she hears it.

Abigail is always pleasant, never unkind. Because of her, he has no worries. Still, it bothers him to see the servants treating her with greater deference than they do him. But she is quick to put him at ease, telling him it is only natural since she is the one who cares for the household. Why should the master bother with such a task when his wife is close at hand?

He doesn't know nor would he care to realize how much energy Abigail expends to keep the peace. Nor does he understand that he is the brunt of frequent jokes. He claims, for instance, that his parents named him Nabal because it means "clever," but everyone else thinks that his name sounds just like the word for "foolish." No doubt Nabal *is* a fool—a grown man with the temperament of a two-year-old.

Though she doesn't show it, Abigail is worn out by her husband's behavior. His constant complaints are a low-grade torture, like continual dripping from a leaky roof. She wonders if perhaps others pity her, thinking she has become like a pretty piece of jewelry adorning the snout of a pig.

She thanks God that at least she has a large household to manage and people to care for. Generous and sensitive, she is a woman who is loved by all. Like her neighbors, Abigail is glad that David is near with his six hundred men. They are encamped in the Desert of Maon, not far from where she and Nabal live. She also knows that Saul would like to kill David. But David is a fox who always gets away.

What she does not know is that ten of David's men are speaking with her husband right now, bearing this message from David: "Long life to you! Good health to you and your household! And good health to all that is yours!

"Now I hear that it is sheep-shearing time. When your shepherds were with us, we did not mistreat them, and the whole time they were at Carmel nothing of theirs was missing. Ask your own servants and they will tell you. Therefore be favorable toward my men, since we come at a festive time. Please give your servants and your son David whatever you can find for them."

David has chosen a season of harvest and plenty to make his request—a time when good men are generous. He expects Nabal to show gratitude for the way he has protected his flocks.

But Nabal has other ideas. Instead of offering provisions to David's army, he seizes the opportunity to prove himself a fool by replying, "Who is this fellow David? Who does this son of Jesse think he is? There are lots of servants these days who run away from their masters. Should I take my bread and my water and my meat that I've slaughtered for my shearers and give it to a band of outlaws who come from who knows where?"

When David hears of Nabal's insulting reply, he is furious. "What a waste to watch over this fellow's property so that nothing goes missing.

Nabal has paid me back evil for good. May God deal with me, be it ever so severely, if by morning I leave alive one male of all who belong to him. Each of you strap on your sword!"

So David and four hundred stout men advance toward Nabal's house in order to take revenge. Meanwhile, Nabal is putting his feet up, taking his ease, and crowing over the size of his harvest.

Sensing danger, one of the servants goes directly to Abigail. "David sent our master his greetings," he tells her, "but he hurled insults at his messengers. Yet these men were very good to us. They never mistreated us, and the whole time we were out in the fields, none of our flock went missing. All night long and every day they were a wall around us. Now think it over and see what you can do, because disaster is hanging over our master and his whole household. He is such a wicked man that no one can talk to him."

Abigail has borne the burden of being married to a fool. But she never imagined a disaster on this scale. Who could have guessed that Nabal's stupidity would outpace his instinct for self-preservation? Unless she intervenes, many members of her household will die. Ordering her servants to collect every bit of food they can put their hands on, she loads up several donkeys, piling them high. There are two hundred loaves of bread, two skins of wine, five slaughtered sheep, sixty pounds of roasted grain, a hundred cakes of raisins, and two hundred cakes of pressed figs. She hopes it will be enough to appease David's wrath. Then she tells her servants, "Go on ahead; I'll follow you." But she says nothing to Nabal.

Risking the dark, Abigail heads out in haste. As she travels, she prays, begging God for deliverance. Before long, she sees David and his men advancing toward her. She hopes he is as good a man as people say he is.

Falling at his feet, she implores him. "My lord, let the blame fall on me alone. Please let your servant speak to you; hear what I have to say.

"Pay no attention, my lord, to that wicked man Nabal. He is just like his name—his name means Fool, and folly goes with him. As for me, your servant, I did not see the men my lord sent. And now, my lord, as surely as the LORD your God lives and as you live, since the LORD has kept you from bloodshed and from avenging yourself with your own hands, may your enemies and all who are intent on harming my lord be like Nabal. And let this gift, which your servant has brought to my lord, be given to the men who follow you."

Taking David's silence as permission to continue, she blesses his future by saying: "The LORD your God will certainly make a lasting dynasty for my lord, because you fight the LORD's battles, and no wrongdoing will be found in you as long as you live. Even though someone is pursuing you to take your life, your life will be bound securely in the bundle of the living by the LORD your God, but the lives of your enemies he will hurl away as from the pocket of a sling. When the LORD has fulfilled for my lord every good thing he promised concerning him and has appointed him ruler over Israel, my lord will not have on his conscience the staggering burden of needless bloodshed or of having avenged himself. And when the LORD your God has brought my lord success, remember your servant."[44]

Her gracious words evoke memories of everything God has promised to David. They also remind him of his first great victory — his triumph over Goliath. He has never heard a woman speak like this, a message that brings peace and hope to his heart, calling him back to God.

"Praise be to the LORD, the God of Israel, who has sent you today to meet me," he says. "May you be blessed for your good judgment and for keeping me from shedding blood and from avenging myself with my own hands. God himself has kept me from harming you. For if you had not come quickly to meet me, not one male in Nabal's household would have been left alive by daybreak. Go home in peace. I have heard your words and granted your request."

It is not yet morning when Abigail arrives home. By now Nabal is drunk and in high spirits. Presiding over a feast, as though he thinks himself a great lord, he's too drunk to listen to what she has to say, so she waits until morning.

Once her husband has sobered up, she tells him everything. His eyes grow wider with each word. His mouth falls open but there are no words — only grunts and moans. Suddenly one side of his mouth droops low, and he collapses on the couch as though he's been turned to stone. Ten days later, God finishes the job, and Nabal is no more.

Oddly, Abigail feels a mixture of sadness and relief. Though she no longer bears the burden of her foolish husband, she senses him every-where as though the misery of his sorry life still lingers.

But David is jubilant when he hears the news, praising God for upholding his cause and keeping him from shedding innocent blood. Wasting no time, he sends word to Abigail, asking her to become his wife.

No one mourns for Nabal.

But everyone honors Abigail. By acting wisely and quickly she has preserved many lives. Though David is still on the run from Saul, she is eager to join him, and so with five of her maids she heads out into the wilderness. There she will marry an outlaw named David, the man she believes will one day be king.

## THE TIMES

Her story takes place about 1005 BC.
*Abigail's story is found in 1 Samuel 25.*

Abigail's household was probably sizeable since her husband was a wealthy landowner whose large herds would have produced a hefty income. Her ability to put her hands on so much food at short notice and the fact that she had servants to command as well as five maids who traveled with her when she married David are further evidence of her wealth.

In most households, women were responsible for threshing and grinding grain, kneading dough, baking bread, cooking, weaving, making clothes, preserving food, and hauling water. It probably took the average woman at least three to four hours every morning simply to grind enough grain for the day's bread. While girls often acted as shepherdesses, some women were so poor that they had to glean in the fields like Ruth or hire themselves out to do fieldwork, work that was normally reserved for men.

Instead of performing these chores herself, Abigail would have had servants who handled them under her direction.

For his part, Nabal would have been responsible for hiring shepherds to care for his large flocks. He would have negotiated a contract that provided them with milk and meat and a certain portion of the wool at shearing time. Though herds sometimes grazed near the household, shepherds often had to lead their flocks a considerable distance in search of pasture. Each shepherd had to provide an accounting for the sheep in his care. Normal birth and attrition rates were carefully calculated, and sheep that had been lost due to predators or illness had to be accounted for by bringing the owner some part of the animal like ears, skin, or tendons. At the end of the day, it was the shepherd's responsibility to make up any losses according to previously agreed terms.

Abigail's life would have changed drastically when she married a warrior who was living with his men and their families in the wilderness. Just prior to the death of Saul and Jonathan, she was kidnapped by a band of raiders along with David's other wife, Ahinoam, as well as many other women and children. Fortunately, Abigail and the others were soon rescued by David and his men. She would likely have been present in David's palace when Michal was returned to him by Ish-Bosheth. Abigail and David had a son named Daniel.

# THE TAKEAWAY

1. What three to five words would you use to describe Abigail's character? Consider especially her actions and her speech to David (1 Samuel 25:24–35).

2. Which of the words you used to describe Abigail represents a quality you wish you had more of in your life? Share the reasons for your response.

3. Abigail is the consummate mediator, effectively brokering peace in the midst of a perilous situation. Have you ever found yourself in a similar situation, putting yourself at risk in some way in order to be a peacemaker? Describe the circumstances and the outcome.

4. Though provoked, neither Abigail nor David takes revenge on Nabal. What does the story reveal about their character and their relationship to God?

# CHAPTER 12

# A Wicked Sorceress

## THE STORY OF THE MEDIUM OF ENDOR

### How a Witch Conjures the Dead

*When thou art come into the land which the LORD thy God giveth thee, thou shalt not learn to do after the abominations of those nations. There shall not be found among you any one that maketh his son or his daughter to pass through the fire, or that useth divination, or an observer of times, or an enchanter, or a witch. Or a charmer, or a consulter with familiar spirits, or a wizard, or a necromancer.*

*For all that do these things are an abomination unto the LORD: and because of these abominations the LORD thy God doth drive them out from before thee.*

Deuteronomy 18:9–12

$\mathcal{D}$oom. He feels it moving toward him though he cannot see it, snarly and bristling with malice. No matter how quickly he moves, pivoting to check his back, he can't seem to get out of its way. He can feel the hair standing up on his neck like hackles on a dog.

It's been like that for some time. Though Saul has men to guard him, he is afraid to close his eyes at night lest he be overtaken.

Some days are worse than others. Today is the worst.

How he longs for a word from God to shatter the darkness. To tell him all is forgiven and that his kingdom will endure. But there is only silence. He should ask the high priest to consult the Urim and Thummim for him, casting lots to discover whether he will prevail against the Philistines who have gathered in great numbers to attack him. But then he remembers that he has already murdered the high priest and many other priests as well. He fears they are in league with David, who has himself gone over to the Philistines.

Perhaps he should summon an interpreter to read his dreams, but these days he has no dreams because he sleeps so little.*

If only he could ask Samuel for a word, but the old man has already been gathered to his fathers and buried in Ramah.

Now there is only silence. No word from God.

Even when God had spoken to him in the past, the words were rarely to his liking. Before Saul had completed the first year of his reign, Samuel had accused him of being a flat out failure. For just a small miscalculation God had rejected him as king. At least Saul thought it was small. He had merely acted when God had told him to wait. But waiting was for women, not for soldiers under the threat of death.

---

* Believing the priests were in league with David, Saul accused them of treachery and executed them. Only Abiather escaped, taking the special ephod, or garment, of the high priest with him. It contained the Urim and Thummim, which he brought to David so that he — and not Saul — could consult the Lord.

For one offense and then another and another, Samuel, on behalf of God, had declared him unfit, saying,

"For rebellion is like the sin of divination,
  and arrogance like the evil of idolatry.
Because you have rejected the word of the LORD,
  he has rejected you as king. "

Though Saul has had his victories, the thing he wants most, he cannot have — to be at peace. To rest secure. After more than forty years of sitting on the throne of Israel, he is still uneasy. Philistines plague him. David eludes him. God abandons him.

He is alone.

The woman is alone too. She is a widow,* doing her best to survive. She lives in Endor, not far from where Saul and his men are encamped. Today she feels restless and unsettled, though she cannot say why. Perhaps it is merely a phase of the moon or the souls of dead men who have gathered to watch the looming battle. She only knows the air is electric. But as always she wants to know more, so she fills a small bowl with water. Then she recites an incantation, asking for wisdom from the world beyond to know which way the fight will go. Carefully she pours a small drop of oil on the water's surface and watches as it splits in two, a sign that great men are about to fall.†

Late in the day, when night has fallen, she is startled to find three strangers at her door. One of them is taller by a head than any man she has ever seen. Pushing through the door, he quickly states his business: "Consult a spirit for me, and bring up the one I name," he says.

But she is no fool. She knows King Saul has strictly forbidden the practice of necromancy, citing the Scripture that says: "If a person turns to mediums and necromancers, whoring after them, I will set my face against that person and will cut him off from among his people." Perhaps these are Saul's men, seeking to entrap her.

---

\* Though the Bible doesn't say she was a widow, the medium of Endor is pictured alone. Since widows had little power to provide for themselves, it is conceivable that one might turn to the practice of sorcery to stay alive despite the dangers.

† Though this scene is not in the Bible, some who practiced divination used this procedure to determine whether an army would prevail or a person would recover from an illness. See "Akkadian Divination," in *The Archeological Study Bible*, ed. Walter C. Kaiser Jr. (Grand Rapids: Zondervan, 2005), 277.

"Surely you know," she replies, "what Saul has done. He has cut off the mediums and spiritists from the land. Why have you set a trap for my life to bring about my death?"

But the big man, the one who had to fold himself in half, stooping low to get through her door, invokes an oath, promising her, "As surely as the LORD lives, you will not be punished for this."

He is such a mixture of earnestness and power that she believes him. "Whom shall I bring up?" she asks.

"Bring up Samuel," he says.

She is good at the art of deception. Since she is the only one who can see the visions and hear the voices she summons from beyond, she need only play her part convincingly. So she speaks in guttural tones, rolls her eyes, and makes her body tremble.

What is so bad about reassuring a mother that her dead child is well, uniting lovers across impassible boundaries, or conveying positive omens to all who seek them? She merely wants to do good, to bring hope, and, yes, to find a way to support herself.

So now she makes a show of asking the reigning powers to raise Samuel up from the grave. But before she can engage in the usual pretense, something terrifying happens. She stares wide-eyed and then looks accusingly at Saul.

"Why have you deceived me? You are Saul!" she exclaims.

"Don't be afraid. What do you see?" the king asks.

"I see a spirit coming up out of the ground."

"What does he look like?"

"An old man wearing a robe is coming up."

Trembling, Saul kneels with his face to the ground.

"Why have you disturbed me by bringing me up?" the old man accuses.

"I am in great distress," Saul tells him. "The Philistines are fighting against me, and God has turned away from me. He no longer answers me, either by prophets or by dreams. So I have called on you to tell me what to do."

Samuel's reply is carried in the throat of the woman of Endor. "Why do you consult me, now that the LORD has departed from you and become your enemy? The LORD has done what he predicted through

me. The LORD has torn the kingdom out of your hands and given it
to one of your neighbors—to David. Because you did not obey the
LORD or carry out his fierce wrath against the Amalekites, the LORD
has done this to you today. The LORD will hand over both Israel and
you to the Philistines, and tomorrow you and your sons will be with
me. The LORD will also hand over the army of Israel into the hands of
the Philistines."

The prophet's words rush at Saul with nightmare force, and he collapses. He is too weak to rise, overcome by fear and hunger, for he has
eaten nothing for a day and a night.

Seeing how shaken he is—and she is shaken too—the witch pleads
with him, saying, "Look, your servant has obeyed you. I took my life in
my hands and did what you told me to do. Now please listen to your
servant and let me give you some food so you may eat and have the
strength to go on your way."

At first Saul refuses. But his men urge him to eat, and he relents.

Slaughtering a fattened calf, the woman quickly prepares it along
with some bread.

After they have eaten, she watches the king and his men depart.
Staring out, she notes a shadow that is darker than the moonlit night.
Hungry and bristling with malice, it trails a little distance behind the
king. She knows that it will not be long until it overtakes him. With a
shudder and a prayer, she closes her door.

## THE TIMES

*Her story probably took place about 1010 BC.*
*The medium of Endor's story is told in 1 Samuel 28.*

Fortune tellers used various means of divination, including observ-
ing patterns of oil dropped into water, interpreting dreams, reading the
stars, and drawing meaning from the entrails of animals.

Though condemned in the Bible (Leviticus 19:31; 20:6) the practice
of necromancy—of attempting to communicate with the dead—was
practiced throughout the ancient Near East, where people employed
magic in an attempt to control their lives by controlling the gods. Such
practices were usually motivated by fear and the desire for power.

By contrast, Israel's all-powerful God could never be controlled, though he could be trusted to watch over those who remained faithful to him. Unlike pagan gods, he communicated, not through secret patterns revealed in the entrails of animals, but through prophets and occasionally through dreams.

At times of national emergency, the Israelites also consulted the Urim and Thummim for revelation. These sacred objects may have been small sticks inscribed with symbols, or they may have been metal objects or stones carried in the breastplate worn by the high priest. They could be cast as lots so that God's will could be ascertained through a series of yes or no questions.

Deuteronomy 18:9–12 indicates that God considered magic an abomination, something his people should shun lest they be defiled by the superstitions of those around them, which could open them up to the influence of false gods and demonic powers.

# THE TAKEAWAY

1. What three to five words would you use to describe the character of the woman of Endor? Consider any positive as well as negative attributes.

2. Have you or has anyone you know ever engaged in the practice of magic? For example, through use of astrology, tarot cards, a Ouija board, or visiting a fortune teller? What motivated you? Were you aware at the time that such practices are off limits for those who believe in God?

3. We know that Saul was desperate to hear something positive from God. What do you think motivated the woman of Endor to try to communicate with the spirit world? How do you think her experience with Saul and Samuel might have affected her?

4. The story showcases how far Saul had fallen. Though a courageous and naturally gifted man, he met a tragic and pathetic end. What does this story reveal about the consequences of trusting yourself more than God?

5. Ancient people believed the supernatural world was real. How is that worldview both affirmed and denied in our culture today? How does your understanding of the existence of the supernatural world shape your daily life?

# CHAPTER 13

# Wicked Desire

## THE STORY OF BATHSHEBA

### How Bathing in Public Caused
### No End of Problems

*Can a man take fire in his bosom,*
*and his clothes not be burned?*

*Can one go upon hot coals,*
*and his feet not be burned?*

*So he that goeth in to his neighbour's wife;*
*whosoever toucheth her shall not be innocent.*

Proverbs 6:27 – 29

$\mathcal{B}$athsheba feels an ache inside, an emptiness so deep she cannot fill it no matter how hard she tries. Her husband, Uriah, is a good man, but he is preoccupied by battles and duty and talks only of warfare. But soldiering bores her. How she wishes he was not merely strong but sensitive, able to enjoy the things she loves, like music and poetry. If only he were home more often. If only he were home right now.

But all the men are gone. They are off fighting the Ammonites, besieging their capital at Rabbah, forty miles northeast of Jerusalem. Curiously, even though it is the spring of the year,* a time when kings march off to battle, David is the only able-bodied man left in the city. Though the king is nearing fifty, he is still good-looking, still remarkably strong. Everyone says so, and Bathsheba agrees.

Because Jerusalem is crowded and compact, built on a mere fifteen acres of land, everyone knows when the king is at home. What's more, her single-story home is close to the palace.

Though it is evening, Bathsheba longs for a fresh breeze to dry the sweat from her brow. Perhaps a bath will cool her down and soothe her restlessness. Like all women, she bathes inside, in the privacy of her home. When Uriah is there, he helps by wetting the sponge and running it back and forth across her back. But since her period has just ended, she will manage the ritual bath by herself as she always does.

She thinks of how refreshing it would be to simply bathe outside in the courtyard. She has never heard of a woman doing such a thing, but why not? Since only the rich can afford multistory homes, there is little danger of nosy neighbors spying her out. There is only the palace to worry about. But what if the king should catch sight of her? Would that be so bad? To have David glimpse her beauty?†

---

* Springtime in the Middle East marks the end of the rainy season, making for passable roads and plenty of fodder for animals.

† Though many commentators cast Bathsheba as an innocent victim, Kenneth Bailey offers

Inside his palace, the king is trying to rest. He sleeps fitfully, perhaps because he cannot stop thinking of the battle raging to the north. Though he is confident of victory, he remembers the toll it takes on the men. God knows how many times he's had to bed down hungry and exhausted, waiting for a city to fall. At least his soldiers are well-provisioned, and they are well-led, too, with Joab in command.

No, it is not anxiety that disturbs his rest but the nagging sense that he should not be sleeping in his soft bed but encamped outside of Rabbah alongside his men. Yet here he is, enjoying a life of ease, while they risk their lives for him. With a sigh, he gets up and begins to stroll around the rooftop garden of his palace.

Despite the fact that Jerusalem is built on a mountaintop, the air is oppressive. David feels it like a damp blanket wrapping him from head to toe. If only lightning would cleave the sky, and a sudden storm would break the heat. Perhaps his restlessness would ease. From his vantage point, he enjoys a commanding view of the Kidron Valley. At twilight, he sees cooking fires glowing in the courtyards below.

Suddenly he catches his breath. His gaze is fixed on a woman, shapely and young. He admires the long, dark hair that cascades in wild tangles down her back. She is bathing inside her courtyard. He watches as she rubs a sponge across her body—caressing her face, her neck, and then her breasts. He knows he should look away. But he has not felt this alive for some time. So he continues to stare.

When she is finished, she suddenly looks up. Is it only his imagination, or is she looking at him the way he has been looking at her? Quickly, before desire fades, he sends a servant to discover who she is.

It doesn't take long to receive the report: "She is Bathsheba, the daughter of Eliam and the wife of Uriah the Hittite."*

The news is disappointing, for the woman he covets is related to men he knows, men who are among his elite troops. The woman's husband is one of his best soldiers. What's more, her grandfather Ahithophel

---

convincing reasons for saying that Bathsheba knew what she was doing when she bathed in clear sight of the palace. See Kenneth E. Bailey, *Jesus through Middle Eastern Eyes* (Downers Grove, IL: InterVarsity Press, 2008), 40–41.

* Uriah was a foreign mercenary who was also a worshiper of the Lord. He is numbered as one of David's thirty mighty men (2 Samuel 23:39; 1 Chronicles 11:41).

is David's personal counselor.* How can he disregard close bonds like these? For a moment he hesitates. But then he recalls her beauty, and he reminds himself that he is king.

Before long, Bathsheba is surprised by a knock at the door. It is the king's men. She knows by the look in their eyes that she cannot refuse to go with them.

When Bathsheba enters the king's private quarters, the two make love, and David tells her she is beautiful beyond all women. Before dawn, she leaves the palace and returns home, and few are the wiser. But it isn't long before she notices the signs. A little cramping, sore breasts, fatigue. She waits until she is certain and then she sends a message to David: "I am pregnant."

These three words will change not only their own lives but the history of Israel, though neither Bathsheba nor David knows it at the time. But both know the law, that adultery is punishable by death. What will the king do?

A few days pass before Bathsheba learns that her husband, Uriah, has been recalled from the front. Relief floods her because she realizes that David has not let the matter go. She plans to welcome Uriah home like a loving wife so no one will suspect the child isn't his. She waits all night, but he never comes. And then the next night, but her husband doesn't return.

She does not know that as soon as he returned to Jerusalem, Uriah was ushered into David's presence.

When the two men embrace, the king inquires about how the battle is going. He wants to know how Joab and his men are faring. Then he sends Uriah away with a gift, encouraging him to spend the night with his wife before returning to the front. It is the least the king can do to honor a faithful soldier.

But Uriah, who is a better man than most, decides to spend the night in the palace rather than returning home. Hearing the news the next day, David is incredulous. "Haven't you just come from a distance? Why didn't you go home?"

---

* If Eliam is the same man mentioned in 2 Samuel 23:34, he was numbered among David's mighty men, and his father would have been Ahithophel.

"The ark and Israel and Judah," Uriah replies, "are staying in tents, and my master Joab and my lord's men are camped in the open fields. How could I go to my house to eat and drink and lie with my wife? As surely as you live, I will not do such a thing!"*

Uriah's words cut David to the bone. Brushing his guilty thoughts aside, he entreats the soldier to stay for just one more day. That night Uriah the Hittite dines with the king, and David gets him drunk. Surely he will not be able to resist spending the night with his beautiful wife. But once again Bathsheba's husband sleeps at the entryway of the palace along with the king's servants and does not return home.

Cursing Uriah as both stubborn and foolish, though he knows him to be the better man, David crafts a plan. Ever the faithful soldier, Uriah returns to the front, carrying a message from David to Joab that will result in his own death. "Put Uriah out in front where the fighting is fiercest," the king tells Joab. "Then withdraw from him so he will be struck down and die."

Though Joab is a hard man, he wonders why David would betray one of his best soldiers. But he is a man under orders, and he will obey the king's command. When the city is under siege, he orders Uriah and a handful of men to the front lines, moving them close to the city walls. Surprised that the enemy has advanced within range of their arrows and spears, the Ammonites slaughter Uriah and everyone with him.

Then Joab sends David an account of the battle, instructing his messenger to beware of the king's anger. "When you have finished giving the king this account of the battle, the king's anger may flare up, and he may ask you, 'Why did you get so close to the city to fight? Didn't you know they would shoot arrows from the wall? Or drop millstones? Why did you get so close to the wall?' If he asks you this, then say to him, 'Moreover, your servant Uriah the Hittite is dead.'"

When the messenger delivers the news, David merely replies, "Say this to Joab: 'Don't let this upset you; the sword devours one as well as another. Press the attack against the city and destroy it.' Say this to encourage Joab."

---

* Whenever David and his men set out for battle, they refrained from having sexual intercourse with their wives as a way of maintaining their ritual purity (1 Samuel 21:4–5).

When Bathsheba hears how her husband has perished, she weeps. And as she mourns, she tries to hide the truth from herself, that half her tears well up from guilt, not grief.

So David, Israel's great hero king, falls prey to lust and then to murder. Though Bathsheba suspects the truth, it will be awhile until she hears the details from David's lips. Meanwhile, she and David marry, and people say this proves the goodness of their king. How generous he is to honor the memory of one of his fallen soldiers by providing his widow with a home. When Bathsheba bears David's son, they say this proves it—that God is smiling on the king and on Uriah's memory.

But if you could stand in heaven and gaze upon God's holy face, you would not detect the slightest hint of a smile. Indeed, while David and Bathsheba's sordid story is unfolding, he is sitting on his great throne, looking down as David strolls the ramparts of his palace. He notes the first spark of desire and then watches it grow into a raging fire that devours the lives of several men. Displeased with David, God speaks to the prophet Nathan about the matter. And here's what Nathan says to David.

"There were two men in a certain town, one rich and the other poor. The rich man had a very large number of sheep and cattle, but the poor man had nothing except one little ewe lamb he had bought. He raised it, and it grew up with him and his children. It shared his food, drank from his cup and even slept in his arms. It was like a daughter to him.

"Now a traveler came to the rich man, but the rich man refrained from taking one of his own sheep or cattle to prepare a meal for the traveler who had come to him. Instead, he took the ewe lamb that belonged to the poor man and prepared it for the one who had come to him."

Enraged, David renders a swift judgment, saying, "As surely as the LORD lives, the man who did this must die! He must pay for that lamb four times over, because he did such a thing and had no pity."

Nathan exclaims in reply:

"You are the man! This is what the LORD, the God of Israel, says: 'I anointed you king over Israel, and I delivered you from the hand of Saul. I gave your master's house to you, and your master's wives into your arms. I gave you all Israel and Judah. And if all this had been too little, I would have given you even more. Why did you despise the word of the LORD by doing what is evil in his eyes? You struck down Uriah the Hittite with the sword and took his wife to be your own. You killed him with the sword of the Ammonites. Now, therefore, the sword will never depart from your house, because you despised me and took the wife of Uriah the Hittite to be your own.'

"This is what the LORD says: 'Out of your own household I am going to bring calamity on you. Before your very eyes I will take your wives and give them to one who is close to you, and he will sleep with your wives in broad daylight.* You did it in secret, but I will do this thing in broad daylight before all Israel.'"

David is devastated. He has become the kind of man he has always despised. Admitting his sin, he learns that he will lose his youngest son, the one Bathsheba has just borne. But it is worse than that. The judgment he rendered against the rich man in Nathan's story will fall upon his own household. Though David will not lose his life, he will be made to "pay for that lamb four times over." In addition to the child Bathsheba has borne, God will allow three more of David's sons — Amnon, Absalom, and Adonijah — to meet untimely deaths, one at the hands of Joab and the others at the hands of their brothers.

As for Bathsheba, no one can say for certain what was in her heart the night she slept with David. Was she powerless against a king's abuse — first raped, then widowed, then rendered childless because of his egregious sin? Or was she a seductress, bent on obtaining a place in David's palace regardless of the cost? Throughout the long years that have transpired since her passing, storytellers have spun the tale both ways.†

What is certain is that before long God blesses her with one more son, a boy who is especially loved by God. She and David name their boy Solomon.

---

* This prophecy was fulfilled when David's son Absalom slept with his father's concubines in a tent erected on the roof of the palace in sight of all. Interestingly, it was Ahithophel, the man who was David's counselor and possibly also Bathsheba's grandfather, who counseled Absalom to undertake this action in order to claim the throne. (See 2 Samuel 16:21–22).

† For an entirely different interpretation of Bathsheba's role in the story, read Ann Spangler and Jean Syswerda, *Women of the Bible* (Grand Rapids: Zondervan, 2007), 176–84.

As Solomon grows, his father's health begins to fail. Eventually David becomes so feeble that he takes to his bed. Shivering violently beneath his covers, he is given a nurse, a beautiful virgin by the name of Abishag to care for and comfort him. Though she and David do not behave as man and wife, she sleeps beside him and keeps him warm.

David's declining health has raised urgent and important questions. Which of his sons will inherit the throne?[*] Deciding that he is the answer to the question everyone is asking, David's son Adonijah conspires with Joab and several others to take power while the king is still alive.

Catching wind of the plot, the prophet Nathan quickly informs Bathsheba, who goes in to David, bowing low before him.

"What do you want?" the king asks.

She says to him, "My lord, you yourself swore to me your servant by the LORD your God: 'Solomon your son shall be king after me, and he will sit on my throne.' But now Adonijah has become king, and you, my lord the king, do not know about it. He has sacrificed great numbers of cattle, fattened calves, and sheep, and has invited all the king's sons, Abiathar the priest and Joab the commander of the army, but he has not invited Solomon your servant. My lord the king, the eyes of all Israel are on you, to learn from you who will sit on the throne of my lord the king after him. Otherwise, as soon as my lord the king is laid to rest with his ancestors, I and my son Solomon will be treated as criminals."

Bathsheba knows that she and Solomon may lose their lives if Adonijah secures the throne. Though David's body is weak, his mind is still strong, and he tells her, "As surely as the LORD lives, who has delivered me out of every trouble, I will surely carry out this very day what I swore to you by the LORD, the God of Israel: Solomon your son shall be king after me, and he will sit on my throne in my place.

"Have Solomon my son mount my own mule and take him down to Gihon. There have Zadok the priest and Nathan the prophet anoint him king over Israel. Blow the trumpet and shout, 'Long live King Solomon!'"[54]

Wasting no time, Zadok and Nathan do as David instructs and Solomon ascends the throne while all the people rejoice.

---

[*] David is probably about seventy years old, while Solomon is about twenty.

As soon as Adonijah hears of it, he begs the king for mercy, and Solomon spares him. But there is one condition. He must abandon his claims to rule. Though Adonijah agrees, he has come too close to power to give up.

One day, shortly after David's death, Adonijah seeks an audience with the queen mother. Surprised to see him, Bathsheba asks him, "Do you come peacefully?"

"Yes, peacefully," he says. And then he continues. "As you know, the kingdom was mine. All Israel looked to me as their king. But things changed, and the kingdom has gone to my brother; for it has come to him from the LORD. Now I have one request to make of you. Do not refuse me. Please ask King Solomon—he will not refuse you—to give me Abishag the Shunammite as my wife."

Bathsheba is no fool.* Though Abishag is still a virgin, everyone in Israel thinks of her as David's wife. To marry the wife of the king is tantamount to proclaiming yourself the king.

Still Bathsheba plays along. "Very well," she says, "I will speak to the king for you."

Wasting no time, she goes to King Solomon and says, "I have one small request to make of you. Do not refuse me. Let Abishag the Shunammite be given in marriage to your brother Adonijah."

She waits for the explosion she knows will follow.

"Why do you request Abishag the Shunammite for Adonijah? You might as well request the kingdom for him—after all, he is my older brother!"

Bathsheba knows that before the sun goes down, her son Solomon will deal with the threat to his throne and that Adonijah will be no more.

When that happens, everything will be as it should be. Her son will rest secure on his throne because she, a mother in Israel, has not shirked back but has risen up to do exactly what needed to be done.

---

* The scene appears in 1 Kings 2:13–25. Though the text does not explicitly state that Bathsheba saw through Adonijah's request, I have spun the story in this direction as Bathsheba must certainly have known that such a marriage would have threatened her son's right to the throne. She would also have known about the shameful episode described in 2 Samuel 16:20–22 in which David's son Absalom tries to usurp the throne by sleeping with the king's harem.

# THE TIMES

*She probably lived sometime between 1050 and 950 BC.*
*Bathsheba's story appears in 2 Samuel 11 – 12 and 1 Kings 1 – 2.*
*She is also mentioned in Matthew 1:6.*

To a greater degree than any of the surrounding peoples, the Israelites possessed detailed laws regarding ritual purity and the methods for restoring it once a person had become ritually unclean. These laws stressed the holiness of God and set out clear stipulations for living in his presence. Since defilement could occur by coming into contact with certain diseases, having sexual intercourse, menstruating, giving birth to a child, eating unclean foods, touching a corpse, having or coming into contact with a bodily discharge, or touching something dead, it was impossible to maintain ritual purity at all times.

In Bathsheba's case, the text makes it clear that she was taking a ritual bath because her period had just ended. By including this detail, the author is making it clear to his readers that David and not Uriah is the father of her child.

Though some commentators cast Bathsheba as co-villain of the story, painting her as a social-climbing seductress, others argue that Nathan's story of the innocent ewe lamb depicts her as the victim of David's crime. They point out that it would have been nearly impossible for her to refuse the king given the extent of his royal power. If this is the case, her story becomes even more tragic because in addition to being raped and having her husband murdered, she suffered the loss of a child because of David's sin.

Instead of being named in Matthew's genealogy of Jesus, she is listed only as "Uriah's wife." Was this Matthew's way of holding his nose when he mentioned the woman he held responsible for David's fall? Or was it one more instance in which Scripture was underlining human sin — in this case, David's sin — and God's gracious provision of a Savior?

Kenneth Bailey, an expert on Middle Eastern New Testament studies who has spent more than forty years living and teaching in the Middle East, says that no self-respecting woman then or now would ever have taken a bath in plain sight of the palace, pointing out that Bathsheba knew exactly what she was doing.

So which is she, villain or victim? We may never know. What we do know is that even the Bible's greatest heroes are fragile characters whose hearts, like ours, are in need of redemption.

Though our culture may see sexual dalliances as naturally occurring behaviors, God sees them in another light because he knows the consequences they wreak on families and on the larger community in which they occur.

## THE TAKEAWAY

1. Read 2 Samuel 11–12. What role do you think Bathsheba played in the story and why?

2. The punishment for adultery was death. Take a few minutes to imagine that you are Bathsheba and that you have just sent a message to King David, telling him you are pregnant. Describe how you are feeling and what you are thinking.

3. Unlike ancient biblical culture, our society often glamorizes adultery and sexual immorality. What are the benefits of resisting the cultural tendencies?

4. Bathsheba had to deal with multiple tragedies—a possible rape, an unwanted pregnancy, the murder of her husband, and the death of her infant son. Yet God blessed her with a son who would become the king of Israel and the world's wisest man. If you had to sum up her life in one sentence, what would you say? If you had to sum up your life thus far in one sentence, what would you say?

5. Describe the progression of David's sin. What do his actions reveal about the consequences of entertaining temptation? How have you seen this process at work in yourself and others?

6. Where in the story do you see evidence of God's goodness and mercy? How have you experienced his mercy with regard to your own failings?

# CHAPTER 14

# Wickedness Personified

## THE STORY OF JEZEBEL

### How the Bad Queen Jezebel Learns It's Not Smart to Fight with God

*The kings of the earth set themselves,*
*and the rulers take counsel together,*
*against the Lord, and against his anointed, saying,*
*Let us break their bands asunder, and cast away their cords from us.*
*He that sitteth in the heavens shall laugh:*
*the Lord shall have them in derision.*
*Then shall he speak unto them in his wrath,*
*and vex them in his sore displeasure.*

Psalm 2:2 – 5

$\mathcal{H}$er lips blush red against skin the color of the seashore. As she walks, you can hear the tinkling of tiny ornaments fastened to feet and ankles. Locks of black curly hair are woven tightly in a braid that snakes halfway down her back with two shorter braids falling at each side. On her wrist is a golden bracelet with a serpent's tail at one end and a lion's head at the other. Back straight, head held high, a gold band encircling her forehead, she is the picture of a wealthy and powerful Phoenician woman. If not for the sly look that dances around her eyes, she would seem quite lovely.

What plot is she hatching now? Not long ago one of her neighbors, a man named Naboth, had been executed on trumped-up charges because Jezebel wanted to confiscate his vineyard to present it as a charming little gift to Ahab,* her husband. While residing at his winter palace in Jezreel, King Ahab had offered to buy Naboth's beautiful vineyard, but the stupid man had refused to sell. Thwarted by this nobody, Ahab had taken to his bed, sulking and refusing to eat.

Astonished that a king would not simply take whatever his heart desired, Jezebel soon hatched a scheme. She arranged for Naboth to be convicted of crimes so grave he would forfeit his life and land. Weeks later, the unlucky man's screams still echo in the minds of those who conspired against him, ignoring his pleas for mercy as he fell under their volley of stones.

Power is a terrible thing in the hands of a wicked person, but it is worse when that person happens to be intensely religious, as Jezebel is. And no wonder. Her daddy is Ethbaal, priest king of Sidon. He serves the Cloud Rider, Storm God, bringer of rain and prosperity. This is the god they call Baal, the one she and her father adore.

---

* Here is what the Bible says about Jezebel's husband: "There was never a man like Ahab, who sold himself to do evil in the eyes of the LORD, urged on by Jezebel his wife. He behaved in the vilest manner by going after idols, like the Amorites the LORD drove out before Israel" (1 Kings 21:25–26).

Just as all royal marriages should be, the marriage of Ahab and Jezebel is a strategic one, giving the Phoenicians access to inland markets while providing Israel with access to the rich markets of the Mediterranean. Despite her rising power, Jezebel has enemies, one in particular. The man's name is Elijah, and, oh, how that wily prophet vexes her.

After marrying Israel's king, Jezebel works hard to sway the hearts of the people away from their God, Yahweh. Determined to establish Baal as Israel's highest reigning deity, she massacres every prophet she can lay her hands on. But some elude her, and the worst of these is Elijah, the meddling fool who claims to have shut up the heavens, causing drought and famine because neither she nor Ahab will kowtow to Israel's God.

Even now, she feels enraged as she recalls the worst of his escapades on what had become the most humiliating day of her life. King Ahab had just returned from Mount Carmel with appalling news.

"Elijah has made us a laughingstock!" he tells her.

Jezebel's old enemy had been at it again, chiding the king for surrendering to his wife's influence and building a temple to Baal: "You have abandoned God, choosing to follow the Baals and making trouble for Israel," Elijah had charged.

What insolence! How could that dog of a prophet dare scold a king?

Ahab continues his sorry tale. "Invite 850 prophets of Baal and Asherah," Elijah told me, "the ones your wife feeds at her table, to meet with me on Mount Carmel. Then we will settle the question once and for all about who God really is — Baal or Yahweh.'

"Bring two bulls, and let the prophets of Baal cut one into pieces and put it on the wood without lighting a fire. Then I will prepare the other bull, laying it on the wood but not lighting a fire. Then let Baal's prophets call on the name of their god, and I will call on the name of mine. The god who answers by fire — he is God."

"It would have seemed weak," Ahab confides to Jezebel, "to refuse his challenge. Plus, I thought it an easy wager, one that could finally rid us of that wild ass of a man.

"So I called the prophets together. They presented their sacrifice on the altar, shouting and dancing around it, praying and imploring:

Baal, God of Thunder,
Storm God who rides upon the clouds,

throw down your lightning bolts,
burn up the offering we have prepared.
Lord of the fertile earth,
greatest of all warrior gods,
vindicate your great name
and show forth your might!

"Surely Baal will answer men of such passion, I thought. We waited … hour upon hour, but nothing happened. No bolt of lightning, not even a spark from heaven.

"I looked over at Elijah, that old fool, and he was shaking with laughter. 'Shout louder!' he yelled. 'Perhaps Baal is sleeping and cannot rouse himself. Or maybe he's away on a trip, or perhaps he has stuffed his ears with cotton.'

"I wanted to slap the look off his face.

"When evening came it was his turn. Incredibly, he began by making the challenge worse—pouring four jars of water on his sacrifice. Elijah drenched everything, not once but three times.

"Imbecile! How stupid you will look when nothing happens," I thought. Then Elijah cried out, invoking the God of Abraham, Isaac, and Israel.

"Suddenly the sky ripped open and fire streaked down, running across the altar and licking up every drop of water in the trench! It consumed the sacrifice, the wood, stones, and even the dirt beneath it."

Recounting the scene, the king struggles to finish. "The people fell on their faces and kept crying out, 'The LORD—he is God! The LORD—he is God!'

"After that Elijah whipped the people into a fury, and they slaughtered the prophets! No one escaped."

Jezebel is trembling, not with fear but with a fury that rushes through her like a surge of power, making her feel invincible. She neither knows nor cares about how Elijah has worked his magic. There is no room in her heart for curiosity, only for vengeance. One thing she does know. The old man must be punished. He cannot be allowed to humiliate her. She will please the lord Baal, upholding his honor as she squashes the man who has troubled them both.

At once, Jezebel dispatches a messenger to Elijah with this threat:

"May the gods deal with me, be it ever so severely, if by this time tomorrow I do not make your life like that of one of the prophets you slew."

As it happens, the gods do deal with Jezebel, but to tell you just how this transpires would be to rush the story.

With the help of an angel, Elijah flees, hiding himself away in the far reaches of the land, and the wicked queen soon realizes that it is impossible to kill a man she cannot find.

Time passes.

But Jezebel remains the same, only more wicked now than she had been, gloating over her most recent triumph—the matter of Naboth and the stolen vineyard.

But the God who sees all things—the God of Abraham, Isaac, and Israel, the one called Yahweh—has his eye on Jezebel and her wicked husband. And this God rouses his servant Elijah, saying, "Go down to meet Ahab king of Israel, who rules in Samaria. He is now in Naboth's vineyard, where he has gone to take possession of it. Say to him, 'This is what the LORD says: Have you not murdered a man and seized his property?…This is what the LORD says: In the place where dogs licked up Naboth's blood, dogs will lick up your blood—yes, yours!'…

"And also concerning Jezebel the LORD says: 'Dogs will devour Jezebel by the wall of Jezreel.'"

King though he is, Ahab hardly dares carry the news of this latest threat back to the queen. To his surprise, Jezebel merely throws back her head and laughs when she hears it. She laughs so long and so hard he thinks she might never stop.

Years pass.

One day Ahab rides out to battle with Jehoshaphat, the king of Judah. "I will enter the battle in disguise," he tells Jehoshaphat, "but you can wear your royal robes." The witless Jehoshaphat does precisely what Ahab instructs.

Meanwhile, their enemy, the king of Aram, instructs his commanders: "Don't fight with anyone, small or great, except Ahab, the king of Israel. As soon as he is finished, the battle will be finished." When the soldiers spot Jehoshaphat, decked out in royal robes, they assume they have found their target. But when Jehoshaphat cries out in his own defense, they realize their mistake. Leaving him alone, they keep up the hunt for Ahab.

Then an archer shoots an arrow, seemingly at random. It sails swift and straight, through long ranks of men, until at last it reaches its target— the disguised king Ahab—piercing him between sections of his armor. Mortally wounded, Ahab screams at his chariot driver, ordering him to flee the fighting. Propped up like a broken banner, the king dies slowly, the life blood draining out of his wound and onto the chariot floor.

Carting the body of their once great king to his palace, his soldiers leave the chariot to be washed in a pool that prostitutes frequent. Then the dogs lick up Ahab's blood just as Elijah's God had foretold.

More years pass.

By now Elijah has gone to heaven and his understudy, Elisha, has taken his place. Though Jezebel's son Joram is reigning in Ahab's place, Elisha gives secret orders for a bold man named Jehu, a commander in Joram's army, to be anointed the new king of Israel.

Elisha appoints an understudy, another prophet to perform this dangerous task. As soon as the man is able to locate Jehu, he whisks him off to an inner room, pours oil onto his head, and then quickly declares: "This is what the LORD, the God of Israel, says: 'I anoint you king over the LORD's people Israel. You are to destroy the house of Ahab your master, and I will avenge the blood of my servants the prophets and the blood of all the LORD's servants shed by Jezebel.... The whole house of Ahab will perish. As for Jezebel, dogs will devour her on the plot of ground at Jezreel, and no one will bury her."

Then the prophet opens the door of the room in which Jehu has just been anointed king and runs for his life.

Wasting no time, Jehu begins marching toward Jezreel where Jezebel's son, Joram, resides. When the lookout at the palace spots him, he calls out, "I see troops coming."

"Get a horseman," Joram orders. "Send him out to meet them and ask, 'Do you come in peace?'"

The horseman rides off to meet Jehu and says, "This is what the king says: 'Do you come in peace?'"

"What do you have to do with peace?" Jehu replies. "Fall in behind me."

The lookout reports, "The messenger has reached them, but he isn't coming back."

So the king sends out a second horseman. When he reaches Jehu and his men, he asks, "Do you come in peace?"

Jehu replies, "What do you have to do with peace? Fall in behind me."

Once again, the lookout reports, "He has reached them, but he isn't coming back either. The driving is like that of Jehu son of Nimshi — he drives like a madman."

"Hitch up my chariot." Then Joram, king of Israel, rides out to meet Jehu. They face each other on the very plot of ground that Jezebel had snatched from Naboth.

"Have you come in peace, Jehu?" Joram asks.

"How can there be peace," Jehu replies, "as long as all the idolatry and witchcraft of your mother Jezebel abound?"

Too late, Joram turns to flee. Jehu draws his bow and shoots him straight between the shoulders. Tossing the body onto the ground, Jehu keeps riding with only a backward glance toward the dead king, whose corpse sprawls awkwardly on the very plot of land that had once belonged to Naboth.

Jehu keeps on riding.

When Jezebel hears he is coming for her, she goes straight to her makeup table. Picking up a silver mirror, she surveys her face, no longer young. The slyness around her eyes has hardened. Lips that had once been round and full pinch together like a slash across her face. With a trembling hand she begins to paint her eyes. Then she brushes her hair. Outwardly calm, she can feel the wild beating of her heart. Arranging her hair, the wicked queen stands by the window, watching as Jehu approaches.

Is she planning to seduce him or resist him? Her attendants do not know.

Her next words make it clear. As soon as Jehu is within earshot, Jezebel shouts: "Have you come in peace, you murderer of your master?" Ignoring the accusation, he treats the queen as though she is a nobody. Looking up at the servants who stand beside her, Jehu shouts: "Who is on my side? Who among you? Throw her down!"

In an instant, the woman who had made herself God's enemy by murdering his prophets and stealing the hearts of those who belong to him tumbles out of the window, landing with a sickening thud upon the ground. There, she is trampled by horses.

Afterward, while Jehu is eating and drinking, recovering from the hard work of committing regicide, it occurs to him that Jezebel ought to be buried. "Take care of that cursed woman and bury her, for she was a king's daughter," he instructs.

But it is too late.

By the time his men reach her, next to nothing of Jezebel is left. Not the purple linen robe she had been wearing, not a single strand of hair. Only a rather small skull, with feet and hands strewn like garbage on the ground.

When Jehu hears the news, he simply shrugs and says: "This is the word of the LORD that he spoke through his servant Elijah. On the plot of ground at Jezreel dogs will devour Jezebel's flesh. Jezebel's body will be like refuse on the ground in the plot at Jezreel, so that no one will be able to say, 'This is Jezebel.'"

Queen Jezebel, whose wickedness was legendary, suddenly ceased to exist. Her evil plots and despicable schemes — what did they come to? Nothing at all. In the end, she and her family perished, and every trace of her was completely wiped out.

Indeed, hers is the fate of all wickedness. Allowed to increase for a time and a season, evil is like a mist that suddenly burns up, vanishing in the heat of the Lord's anger, never to be seen again.

So ends the story of the Bible's most wicked queen, an exceptionally devoted woman who discovered, rather too late, that it simply doesn't pay to fight with God.

## THE TIMES

Her story takes place during the period 873 – 841 BC.
*Jezebel's story is drawn from 1 Kings 16:29 – 33;*
*18:1 – 19:2; 21:1 – 25; 2 Kings 9.*

After Solomon's death, the tribes of Israel became divided in two, with Israel in the north and Judah in the south. Jezebel and Ahab's story unfolds in Israel.

One of the strongest female characters in the Bible, she is also one of the few women who is depicted as entirely evil. As a show of contempt, the biblical writer deliberately distorts her Phoenician name, which means, "the prince Baal exists," replacing it with a Hebrew name that conveys a not-so-subtle insult. The Hebrew word means, "Where is the excrement (manure)?"

In addition to slaughtering Israel's prophets, Jezebel actively promoted Baal worship, using her considerable wealth to support 450 prophets of Baal and 400 prophets of Asherah, the female consort of the Canaanite god, El.

An ancient seal, which may have belonged to Jezebel and which is inscribed with her name in Phoenician script, was discovered in Samaria, where she and Ahab ruled. Though she and Elijah were bitter enemies, the battle on Mount Carmel represented the climax of an ongoing war for supremacy, not merely between two human beings, but between Yahweh and Baal.

Considered a god of storms and fertility, Baal was widely worshiped throughout the region and was called by various names, like Baal Hadad, Baal Hamon, or Baal Melqart, depending on the location. In a polytheistic society, people believed that the gods operated within a hierarchical structure. Powerful, ruling deities were associated with certain nations while lesser deities were connected to clans and families. Ahab and Jezebel may have been attempting to replace Yahweh with Baal as Israel's national God.

Unlike most of Ahab's prophets, Elijah was not in the employ of the king. As Yahweh's spokesman, he broke ranks with other prophets in the region, whose job it was to flatter the king and legitimize his rule. Instead of paying lip service to Ahab and Jezebel, Elijah repeatedly risked his life to strike at the heart of royal power. He knew that idolatry would destroy his people because they would become like the idols they worshiped rather than like the holy God who had chosen them for his own.

# THE TAKEAWAY

1. The root of Jezebel's wickedness was embedded in idolatry, which is a distorted form of worship. Idolatry consists of giving primacy to something or someone other than God. In what subtle and not-so-subtle ways do you recognize idolatry in contemporary culture? What forms might it take not only in the wider world, but also among those in your community, including the Christian community?

2. What does the lopsided battle between Jezebel's 450 prophets and the lone prophet Elijah say about the nature of spiritual power? How have you experienced God's power at work in your own life despite the odds against you?

3. What kinds of things tend to function as potential idols in your life—someone or something other than God to which you ascribe ultimate worth? For example, it might be a longed-for relationship, a certain income level or standard of living, a desired possession, or even allegiance to a particular political party. In what ways, small or large, does this someone or something turn your heart away from God?

4. Years passed before Ahab and then Jezebel faced God's promised judgment. In the meantime, Jezebel may have lulled herself into thinking she had defied God without consequences. How is her story a cautionary tale about what happens to those who defy God, whether brazenly or more subtly, as sometimes happens today?

# CHAPTER 15

# Wickedly Wayward

## THE STORY OF GOMER

### How a Prodigal Wife Learns
### the Meaning of True Love

*For thy Maker is thine husband; the LORD of hosts is
his name; and thy Redeemer the Holy One of Israel;
The God of the whole earth shall he be called.*

Isaiah 54:5

$S$he stands outside in the cool, refreshing rain, allowing it to run in rivulets across her cheeks and down her lips. She is like the lily of the valley that spreads its fragrance across the fields or like the lush, abundant grapes that make men glad. Fertility and fruitfulness, celebration and wild abandon—these are the forces that rise and surge within her.

Young, beautiful, and bold, she is always smiling, flashing her big, dark eyes, attracting inevitable attention. God knows how easy it would be to entice her admirers into showering her with gifts of silver and gold. Though she is determined to squeeze every ounce of sweetness from life, that's not all she wants. More than anything, she is looking for someone she can adore.

Suddenly she notices a man hurrying toward her. It is not desire that propels him but pain and hurt. She knows this because she is good at reading people and because it is her husband who draws near.

"Gomer," he says, "Come home!"

And so she does, but reluctantly. Hosea is a good man, but goodness can be boring. He talks only of God and of faithfulness to the covenant, dampening her high spirits and making her feel ashamed of her sins. But how can it be wrong to dream of having just a little pleasure in this life?

Hosea is distressed by all he sees. The people offer sacrifices at pagan shrines, praising Baal for every harvest. They have forgotten the faith their fathers professed. But she thinks it matters little how people name their gods—whether Baal or Yahweh or even Yahweh's presumed wife Asherah—as long as they acknowledge god by paying homage for the rain and the harvest, the bread and the wine. If Yahweh is so upset, why has the rain been so abundant, the crops so lush, and the peace so prolonged? If everyone is worshiping the wrong god, why have so many people been blessed with so much?

But Hosea insists on pointing out the twistedness in everything— the gap between rich and poor, all the deception and lies, the sleeping around, the killings, and the worship of countless idols. He says God's people have become no different than the Canaanites. Instead of whispering his disapproval, he shouts it, as though he is God's chosen mouthpiece, telling everyone—especially the priests—that they are harlots and whores and that God will surely punish them.

She finds it infuriating and embarrassing to be known as the wife of the prophet Hosea, and her eyes begin to cast about for someone she can truly love.

If Gomer would stop for just one moment and try to read her husband's heart, she would discover that she has broken it more than once. Perhaps she already knows this. But she doesn't know—not yet—how hard it was for Hosea to betroth himself to her. She has no inkling that Yahweh, the God of his ancestors and hers, had instructed him, saying, "Go, marry a promiscuous wife and have children with her, like an adulterous wife this land is guilty of unfaithfulness to the LORD." Nor does she realize that her marriage has become a public parable—a story God is telling to his people.

Already she has borne three children. The first was a boy her husband named Jezreel, meaning "God scatters."* Then came a girl he named Lo-Ruhamah, meaning "not loved," and another son he named Lo-Ammi, which means "not my people." Though he hasn't said as much, she knows he doubts the last two babies are his.

Yet every time he thunders on about doom and destruction, her prophet-husband can't stop himself from adding just a little note of hope: "The Israelites will be like the sand on the seashore, which cannot be measured or counted. In the place where it was said to them, 'You are not my people,' they will be called 'children of the living God.' The people of Judah and the people of Israel will come together; they will appoint one leader and will come up out of the land, for great will be the day of Jezreel."

Gomer knows that Jezreel, which is the name of a large and fertile valley north of Samaria, has more than one meaning. Instead of "God scatters," it can also mean "God sows," signifying that after the coming

---

* Jezreel was where Jehu assassinated Jezebel, Joram, and Jezebel's remaining sons, thereby wiping out the line of Ahab. Through Hosea, God declared that he would punish Jehu's dynasty for their overzealous brutality and for their continued tolerance and promotion of Baal worship.

judgment God will once again provide for his people in this lush and beautiful land.

But she is sick of listening to all his dire warnings and dark pronouncements, and so she leaves Hosea and abandons her children. Throwing off every constraint, she begins to lead a life of dissolution. For a while it pleases her. She does what she wants when she wants to do it. Her lovers say nothing disagreeable but only what she longs to hear, that she is the most stunning and exciting woman they have known. She feels enriched by all the gifts they give, silver and gold, wool and linen, wine and oil. But something still is missing.

That something turns out to be someone — a man she meets whose charms are even greater than her own. She loves to lean against his massive chest and feel his strong, encircling arms. A man of influence and quick wit, her lover knows exactly what will please her. As long as he is near, she feels secure. As long as she reveres him, he is glad to stay.

But things begin to turn. He is away more than she likes, and he is not always as attentive as he should be. She begins to cling to him and then to quiz him about where he's been and who he's been with. The more she asks, the less he tells. The more she pursues, the more he runs away until at last he vanishes.

Left alone, she feels her emptiness. Though she tells herself her lover will soon return, her tears reflect the truth — that he is gone forever. As time passes, she begins to realize that loneliness is not her only problem. The world around her is changing rapidly. For many years, King Jeroboam II presided over Israel. Now the king is dead, and the country is descending into chaos. Life becomes more difficult as one king is murdered and another is quickly crowned.

Gomer is changing too. She is growing older. Many of the men who seek her services now seem rough and coarse. When their business is done, they do not linger. In these uncertain times, she has no one to cheer her when she becomes depressed or to care for her when she falls ill. Instead of solid rock beneath her, there is only shifting sand.

And there is disease, sores that come and do not heal. Applying layers of makeup, she does her best to conceal the worry that etches itself in tiny lines around her eyes. Fatigue creeps over her like a stubborn fog that will not lift.

By now, her stores of silver and gold have shrunk. She spent freely at first but now penuriously because a few coins are all that's left between her and the shelterless streets. On the nights when no one visits, she sits alone, remembering the haunting words her husband spoke the day she left. She can still hear the rage in his voice and see the angry tears roll down his face.

> "Rebuke your mother, rebuke her,
>     for she is not my wife,
>     and I am not her husband.
> Let her remove the adulterous look from her face
>     and the unfaithfulness from between her breasts.
> Otherwise I will strip her naked
>     and make her as bare as on the day she was born;
> I will make her like a desert,
>         turn her into a parched land,
>         and slay* her with thirst."

Though spoken a lifetime ago, Hosea's words have finally found their mark. She knows what he was talking about. To be abandoned, rejected, cast off like you are nothing. Surely there can be no greater pain.

But then his words turn tender for he speaks of transforming the Valley of Achor (meaning "trouble") into a door of hope. But what kind of magic can turn a person's troubles into hope? This she does not know.

> I will betroth you to me forever, he says.
>     I will betroth you in righteousness and justice,
>         in love and compassion.
>     I will betroth you in faithfulness,
>         and you will acknowledge the Lord.

As the words sink in, she feels their sting more than their promise. She has lost too much — thrown it all away. Even though she longs for home and husband and children, she lacks the courage to return. Instead, she spends the last of her treasure and falls into debt. Unable to pay the interest, she sells herself into slavery. Still young, her future stretches out in endless wretchedness.

---

* According to the letter of the law of the day, Hosea could have had Gomer executed for her unfaithfulness, though punishment was rarely carried to that extreme.

And then one day, a man comes looking for her. Her man comes looking for her. Hosea has cash in hand, all the money he can scrape together. When he finds he doesn't have enough, he throws some barley into the deal. And she is freed.

But what will she do with her freedom?

Later he tells her what happened. "The LORD came to me," he explains, "and told me to take you as my wife, saying 'Go, show your love to your wife again, though she is loved by another and is an adulteress. Love her as the LORD loves the Israelites, though they turn to other gods and love the sacred raisin cakes.'*

"So I bought you for fifteen shekels of silver and twelve bushels of barley. You are to live with me many days; you must not be a prostitute or be intimate with any man, and I will live with you."

So Gomer, who has lived a dissolute life, returns home to live with Hosea, a husband she does not deserve. But what has become of her children? You will be glad to learn that Lo-Ruhamah is now Ruhamah, meaning "loved," and Lo-Ammi is called Ammi, meaning "my people."

But what of Israel? Transfixed by the story of the prophet and the prostitute, God's people fail to see how it could possibly apply to them. So they continue on their reckless, wayward course.

After a short while, God allows a king to rise up in the north. Before long, this mighty, pagan king crushes Israel, carrying its people captive. Separated from their own land, the land God gave to them, his people become as insubstantial as the morning mist, like a bit of smoke escaping through a window. But God, who wastes nothing, uses their hardships to call them to their senses. In time, they remember the wonderful story of Gomer and Hosea, and the words of the prophet, who said:

"Come, let us return to the LORD.
   He has torn us to pieces
   but he will heal us;
he has injured us
   but he will bind up our wounds.
After two days he will revive us;
   on the third day he will restore us,
   that we may live in his presence.

---

* Hosea 3:1; note that people offered raisin cakes to Baal in thanksgiving for a good harvest.

Let us acknowledge the LORD;
   let us press on to acknowledge him.
As surely as the sun rises,
   he will appear;
he will come to us like the winter rains,
   like the spring rains that water the earth."

Like Gomer, who suffered greatly for betraying the only man who truly loved her, God's people languish in a land that is not their own. But when at last they turn to God, he comes to them just as he said he would—like the winter rains, and like the spring rains that water the earth. He bends down from heaven to bless and provide, betrothing himself to them forever in righteousness and justice, in love and compassion. Only then do they discover how deeply they are loved.

## THE TIMES

Her story takes place sometime between 755 – 722 BC.
*Gomer's story is found in Hosea 1 – 3.*

After Solomon's death, David's kingdom became divided, with Israel in the north and Judah in the south. As one commentator describes the situation, Israel and Judah "were like two cats living in an alley with one tiger named Egypt living at one end and another named Assyria at the other, each scrapping for control over the laneway."*

Gomer and Hosea's story unfolded on the northern end of that alley, in the kingdom of Israel. When Hosea first began to prophesy, Israel enjoyed a period of relative affluence and political stability. As life became easier, the nation had moved away from God, adopting many of the religious and cultural practices of the Canaanites, including Baal worship.

Since the Israelites depended on rain for a good harvest, the temptations of Baal worship with its stress on the bringing of rain and fertility proved too much for many people to resist. Even though Elijah had dealt a huge blow to Jezebel and the prophets of Baal in the previous century, many people still combined Baal worship with the worship of

---

* J. Glen Taylor, "Hosea," *Zondervan Illustrated Bible Backgrounds on the Old Testament*, ed. John H. Walton (Grand Rapids: Zondervan, 2009), 5:6.

Yahweh, no doubt considering themselves God's faithful followers even though they were behaving more like followers of Baal.

After the death of Jeroboam II (a descendant of Jehu, the man responsible for Jezebel's death), Israel's prosperity began to decline. Ruled by a succession of weak kings, it became politically unstable at the same time that Assyria was gaining strength in the north.

Throughout their history, God had promised to protect his people if only they stayed close to him. Sadly, both kingdoms strayed. As a consequence, Israel fell to Assyria in 722 BC and Judah to Babylon in 587 BC.

## THE TAKEAWAY

1. Why do you think God asked Hosea to take the radical step of marrying a woman other men would have despised?

2. Why was it so hard for Israel to listen to what God was saying?

3. Even strong marriages can have their difficulties. Comment on the challenges inherent in a marriage between God and his people, between God and you.

4. Though Gomer practiced a flagrant form of unfaithfulness, it's possible to be unfaithful in ways that are less obvious. We can become devoted to having a perfect relationship, a perfect job, or perfect health, for instance. Discuss episodes in your own life when you were tempted to put someone or something before your relationship with God. What were the circumstances? How did you deal with them?

5. When God spoke about betrothing himself to his people, he spoke of a relationship that would be characterized by righteousness and justice on the one hand and love and compassion on the other. What does this mean in practical terms? As part of your reflections, consider recent examples from your own life in which you experienced the tension between righteousness and compassion.

6. When Gomer's story begins, God's people are behaving like everyone around them. Discuss the similarities and differences between her culture and ours.

# CHAPTER 16

# Wicked Funny

## THE STORY OF ESTHER

### How a Good Queen
### Gets the Last Laugh

*But if thou shalt indeed obey his voice, and do all that
I speak; then I will be an enemy unto thine enemies,
and an adversary unto thine adversaries.*

Exodus 23:22

$O$nce upon a time in a faraway land in a city called Susa,* at the winter palace of King Xerxes, three splendid feasts are held. The first of these lasts for 180 days—a full half year. It gathers together the leading men of Persia so that the king can enlist their support for his coming campaign against the Greeks. While the men strategize and plot about the merits of the planned invasion, they have ample time to marvel at the riches† of the court and the splendor of the king, who adorns himself each day in scarlet-colored trousers and robes of shimmering purple.

Once the king is confident of their unqualified support, he holds another feast. This one lasts for seven days and is open to every man in the citadel of Susa—from the least to the greatest.

Please don't imagine that the king and his guests are confined to a room within the royal palace. Instead they feast outside in the sumptuous garden that adjoins it, drinking wine to their heart's content while they recline on softly cushioned couches that are made of solid gold. Streams of water cascade through long rows of stately trees and plantings artfully arranged in geometric shapes. Colonnaded pavilions paved in multicolored mosaics are decorated with white and blue linen cloths that hang from silver rings on marble pillars. Filled with every known species of plant and animal, the king's garden offers every guest a taste of paradise.‡

On the seventh day of the feast, when the king is in high spirits, he commands the seven eunuchs who serve him to bring before him Queen Vashti, wearing her royal crown. He plans to parade her in all her loveliness before his honored guests because the queen's beauty will provide yet more evidence of the greatness of his splendor.

---

* Susa is located in what is now southwestern Iran.

† Persia was extremely wealthy. The Greek historian Herodotus indicated that Xerxes' father, King Darius, received more than 14,000 talents of gold and silver in annual tribute, which would amount to nearly 800,000 pounds of these precious metals.

‡ The Persians created sumptuous gardens, calling them *paridaida*, which literally translates as "beyond the wall," referring to an enclosed area. The Greek word *paradeisos*, which becomes "paradise" in English, is derived from this word.

But Vashti is not a particularly compliant queen. Plus, she is busy hosting a female-only feast* inside the royal palace. Like her husband, she has been eating and drinking for several days. When the queen hears of the king's command, she is indignant. Who does he think he is, ordering her to parade around before hordes of drunken men as though she is nothing but a prized cow? Emboldened by one too many cups of royal wine,† the queen does the unthinkable. She refuses.

Odd though it seems, the Persians think they are wisest whenever they are inebriated.‡ Today Xerxes is drunk, which makes him want to boast and preen. It also makes his temper flare.

As soon as he learns of his wife's refusal, he explodes. And he is not the only one. His counselors are indignant. How dare a woman upset the natural order of things? Even if she is the queen, this is simply too much for any man to bear. What will their own wives think when they hear the queen has refused to obey the king? There will be no end of disrespect and discord. It is outrageous — and terrifying. So the king and his counselors conspire together with all their might to put down a revolt that hasn't even begun.

On the advice of his counselors, Xerxes issues a decree deposing Vashti and affirming — lest any woman doubt it — that every man is always and everywhere to be considered the sole ruler of his household.

Emboldened by this great domestic victory, Xerxes travels west to lead what will become a failed invasion of Greece while his commissioners begin looking for Vashti's replacement. She will be chosen from among the realm's most beautiful virgins, a woman of impeccable character who will never dare contradict the king. Throughout the kingdom a search is made, and the most beautiful young women are transported to the harem of the king. One of these is Esther, a young Jewish woman, an orphan who has been lovingly raised by her cousin Mordecai.

Like the other young women who have been gathered like fish

---

* Though Xerxes and Vashti are hosting separate feasts, it was common among the Persians for men and women to feast together.

† Though the Bible doesn't indicate that Vashti was drinking, it is not an unlikely conjecture given the fact that she was holding her own feast at the time the king summoned her to appear at his.

‡ The Greek historian Herodotus indicated that decisions that were made when the king and his counselors were sober had to be revisited when they were inebriated to ensure that they were still judged to be sound. Apparently the Persians believed that intoxication brought them closer to the spirit world, which would in turn bring them closer to enlightenment.

into Xerxes' net, she is entrusted to the eunuch in charge of his harem. Esther is so winsome that she soon becomes his favorite. Assigning her the best spot in the harem, he lavishes her with special foods, servants, and beauty treatments.

Meanwhile, Mordecai instructs Esther not to breathe a word about her Jewish identity. No one, not even the king, is to know she is a Jew.

Before she can marry the king, Esther must complete twelve months of beauty treatments, six months with oil of myrrh and six with perfumes and cosmetics. During this time, she must also learn palace protocol so she can behave as a wife of the king should. When the time comes, she will be called to the king's bed chambers, where they will consummate their union, and she will become one of his many wives. Once summoned, she may not return to him again without his expressed request.

One night after the king has finally returned from Greece, Esther is called to his chambers. The king is so taken with her that he sets a crown upon her head and makes her queen instead of Vashti. To celebrate her ascendancy to the throne, a banquet is held in her honor and a holiday proclaimed throughout the provinces.

But this is not yet the happy conclusion to her story. For that will take some time.

After a while, her cousin Mordecai uncovers a wicked plot, which he makes known to Esther. It seems that two of the king's officers are planning to assassinate Xerxes. When Esther tells the king, the two men are promptly executed. Though Mordecai's good deed is dutifully recorded in the book of the annals, it is promptly forgotten.

About this time, the king elevates a despicable man by the name of Haman to the highest office in the land. An Amalekite* by birth, his ancestry traces back to ancient enemies of the Jewish people. Though all the royal officials kneel in homage to Haman, Mordecai alone refuses to bow down. Full of self-importance, Haman is enraged by Mordecai's refusal. Instead of deciding to punish only Mordecai, as one might expect a normal man to do, he decides to wipe out all the Jews of Persia.

---

* The Amalekites were descendants of Esau. During Saul's reign in Israel, God instructed him to wipe out the Amalekites and take none of their goods. Instead Saul spared their king and kept some of the plunder. His disobedience cost him his throne (1 Samuel 15).

Haman knows that a plan this devious must not be carried out without first consulting the gods. So he casts the *pur* (the lot). Tossing a small clay cube onto a surface on which the months and days of the year have already been drawn, he notes as it lands on an auspicious date, eleven months into the future.

Having fixed the exact day for executing his wicked plan, Hamn goes straight to the king with a false report about the Jews. "A certain people," he tells Xerxes, "are scattered throughout your empire. They are a peculiar people with their own habits and customs, and they refuse to obey the king's laws. Why should the king tolerate them?"

Then he proposes a strategy for wiping them out, sweetening the deal with an enormous bribe. "If it pleases the king, let a decree be issued to destroy them, and I will put ten thousand talents of silver into the royal treasury for the men who carry out this business."

Since ten thousand talents amounts to most of what comes into the royal treasury during the course of a single year, the king readily agrees. No doubt Haman is planning to raise the money by plundering the wealth of his intended victims.

So the royal secretaries waste no time in writing up a decree for the king to sign. On the thirteenth day of the twelfth month, the month of Adar, it will be permissible to destroy, kill, and annihilate the Jews — young and old, women and little children. Anyone who wants to may slaughter them and plunder their goods on that day.

When Mordecai hears of the king's decree, he tears his clothes and begins to mourn. Sending word to Esther, he tells her exactly what Haman is plotting and how much money he has promised the king. Then he urges her to go to the king and beg for mercy on behalf of her people.

But Esther hesitates. Even though she has been queen for five years, she is still afraid of Xerxes' mercurial temper. So she sends this response to Mordecai: "All the king's officials and the people of the royal provinces know that for any man or woman who approaches the king in the inner court without being summoned the king has but one law: that they be put to death unless the king extends the gold scepter to them and spares their lives. But thirty days have passed since I was called to go to the king."

She fears her appeal with the king may already have worn thin.

But Mordecai sends back this reply: "Do not think that because you are in the king's house you alone of all the Jews will escape. For if you remain silent at this time, relief and deliverance for the Jews will arise from another place, but you and your father's family will perish. And who knows but that you have come to your royal position for such a time as this?"

Esther responds by asking Mordecai to mobilize all the Jews in Susa to begin a fast. "Do not eat or drink for three days, night or day," she instructs. "I and my maids will fast as you do. When this is done, I will go to the king, even though it is against the law. And if I perish, I perish."

On the third day, weakened by the fast and terrified by what her husband may do, Esther puts on her royal robes, and then enters the presence of the king. Will he raise his golden scepter and spare her life, or will he cast it down and condemn her to death?

She does not know.

But then she sees the light in his eyes and the smile that quickly spreads across his face. The king is pleased to see her! Holding out his golden scepter, King Xerxes calls her forward. "What is it, Queen Esther? What is your request? Even up to half the kingdom, it will be given you," he says.

"If it pleases the king," she replies, "let the king, together with Haman, come today to a banquet I have prepared for him."

So that night the king and Haman feast together with the queen. As they drink their wine and take their ease, Xerxes turns to Esther and asks, "Now what is your petition? It will be given you. And what is your request? Even up to half the kingdom, it will be granted."

But Esther senses that the time is not yet ripe. Rather than asking the king to publicly admit his mistake by revoking his own decree, she replies, "If the king regards me with favor, let the king and Haman come tomorrow to the banquet I will prepare for them. Then I will answer the king's question."

So the king and Haman depart. By now, Haman's head is filled with visions of greatness. Even the queen has exalted him by inviting him not once but twice to dine alone with her and the king. But his dreams of glory are shattered as soon as he encounters Mordecai, that insolent Jew, who once again refuses to bow down and pay him homage. By the time Haman arrives home, he is seething. Telling his wife and friends exactly what has happened, he listens as they offer their advice:

"Build a gallows seventy-five feet high and ask the king in the morning to impale* Mordecai on it. Then go and enjoy yourself, feasting with the king and queen, knowing that your enemy is no more."

"Wonderful!" Haman replies, clapping his hands in glee.

That night, while Haman is busy arranging for a gallows to be built near his home, it just so happens that the king is tossing and turning in his bed, unable to sleep. To pass the time he orders the book of the chronicles, the record of his reign, to be brought in and read to him. The book is opened to the precise page that recounts the story of how Mordecai once saved his life.

"What honor has been given to Mordecai for uncovering the plot against me?" the king inquires. When he learns that Mordecai has never been rewarded for his loyalty, he asks his attendant if any of his officials are present in the palace. As it happens, Haman has just crossed into the outer court. Eager for revenge, he has come early to seek the king's blessing on his plan to execute Mordecai. But before he can pose his question, the king inquires: "What should be done for the man the king delights to honor?"

This is a pleasant surprise, thinks Haman. Surely there is no one the king would rather honor than me. So he replies: "For the man the king delights to honor, have them bring a royal robe the king has worn and a horse the king has ridden, one with a royal crest placed on its head. Then let the robe and horse be entrusted to one of the king's most noble princes. Let them robe the man the king delights to honor, and lead him on the horse through the city streets, proclaiming before him, 'This is what is done for the man the king delights to honor!'"

"Go at once," the king commands Haman. "Get the robe and the horse and do just as you have suggested for Mordecai the Jew, who sits at the king's gate. Do not neglect anything you have recommended."

---

* Though some translations of the Bible indicate that Haman was planning to hang Mordecai, the Persian practice was to impale victims on wooden stakes. So it seems likely that the victim was first executed and then was hung or impaled on the gallows for all to see. See Anthony Thomasino, "Esther," *Zondervan Illustrated Bible Backgrounds on the Old Testament*, ed. John H. Walton (Grand Rapids: Zondervan, 2009), 3:486.

So Haman, who has prided himself on reaching the pinnacle of power, suddenly feels as though he has been plunged into the depths. He has no choice but to obey the king's order. Placing a royal robe on Mordecai, he leads him on horseback through the city streets, proclaiming: "This is what is done for the man the king delights to honor!"

Afterward Haman rushes home. When his wife and friends learn how Haman has been shamed, they tell him the truth: "Since Mordecai, before whom your downfall has started, is of Jewish origin, you cannot stand against him — you will surely come to ruin!" While they are still talking, Haman is summoned to the banquet that Queen Esther has prepared.

While Esther, Xerxes, and Haman are drinking their wine from golden goblets, each one different than the other, the king inquires of Esther once again, assuring her he will grant her request, whatever it may be.

"If I have found favor with you, Your Majesty, and if it pleases you, grant me my life — this is my petition," she says. "And spare my people — this is my request. For I and my people have been sold to be destroyed, killed and annihilated. If we had merely been sold as male and female slaves, I would have kept quiet, because no such distress would justify disturbing the king."

As soon as he hears it, the king erupts: "Who is he? Where is he — the man who has dared to do such a thing?"

"An adversary and enemy!" Esther declares. "This vile Haman!"

Enraged, the king puts down his goblet and stalks out of the room. Though Haman knows it is a capital offense for a man to remain in the royal harem without the presence of the king or one of his eunuchs, he stays behind to beg Queen Esther for his life. Falling on the couch on which she is reclining, he is still pleading with her when the king re-enters the room.

Exploding with rage Xerxes exclaims, "Will he even molest the queen while she is with me in the house?"

After Haman is arrested, one of the eunuchs says to the king, "A gallows seventy-five feet high stands by Haman's house. He had it made for Mordecai, who spoke up to help the king."

"Hang him on it!" the king commands.

So wicked, vile, vainglorious Haman falls victim to the punishment he had intended for Mordecai. With his body swinging high up in the air, he becomes a spectacle for everyone to see.

That very day, the king hands Haman's estate over to the queen, who then appoints Mordecai to administer it. But this is not yet the happy conclusion to Queen Esther's amazing story, for the king's decree to annihilate the Jews cannot be revoked.

Falling on her knees and weeping copiously, Esther pleads with King Xerxes once more, begging him to put an end to Haman's evil plot. "If it pleases the king," she says, "and if he regards me with favor and thinks it the right thing to do, let an order be written overruling the dispatches that Haman ... devised and wrote to destroy the Jews in all the king's provinces. For how can I bear to see disaster fall on my people? How can I bear to see the destruction of my family?"

Though the king does not retract the initial decree, which allows the Jews to be slaughtered on the thirteenth day of the twelfth month, the month of Adar, he is willing to issue another. With Mordecai's help he draws up a decree that allows the Jewish people to assemble an army with which to destroy, kill, and annihilate the men of any nationality or province who might attack them and their women and children. It also gives them permission to plunder the goods of their enemies.

After this is done, the king adorns Mordecai in royal garments of blue and white, dressing him in a purple robe of fine linen and placing a large crown of gold upon his head. Because of Mordecai's rise, Haman's demise, and the new decree empowering the Jews, the entire empire is seized with fear of them, and many people become Jews. Then Susa holds a great feast in order to celebrate.

The thirteenth day of the twelfth month, the month of Adar,* becomes an auspicious day for all the Jews of Persia. On the very day their enemies had planned to annihilate them, the Jews strike with deadly force, wiping out all those who hate them.

From that day forward, Queen Esther and Mordecai are honored as heroes among God's people. Every year a celebration, called Purim†

---

* February or March 473 BC.

† Jews throughout the world still celebrate Purim, a holiday that involves some initial fasting and in which the book of Esther is read. People dress up in masks and costumes, reenact the story,

(meaning "lots"), is held so that every generation and every family without fail can celebrate how the Jews were delivered. On that day there is a great deal of feasting and nonstop laughter when they remember how that stupid, wicked Haman was bested by the good Queen Esther and her cousin, Mordecai the Jew.

## THE TIMES

*Her story takes place from 483 to 473 BC.*
*Esther's story is found in the book of Esther.*

The events recounted in the book of Esther took place after Babylon conquered Judah in 587 BC. After that, Cyrus the Great, king of Medea and Persia, conquered Babylon in 538 BC, and the territory reverted to him. Though Cyrus issued a decree allowing Jews who'd been taken into captivity to return to Judah, many decided to remain in the land where they had settled. Some had moved eastward to Susa, the winter capital of the Persian Empire.

Esther and Mordecai were part of a Jewish community that remained faithful to their religious and cultural heritage. By then, Cyrus's grandson, Xerxes (also known as Ahasuerus), was reigning as king.

Though Persia was a patriarchal society in which wives were expected to obey their husbands, women were not generally oppressed and often worked as business managers, who at times also supervised men.[*]

Eunuchs (castrated male servants) were highly prized in the ancient Near East. Because they were unable to father children, they were trusted to watch over royal harems. They could hold positions of great power since no one would suspect them of scheming to establish a dynasty of their own. Persian monarchs valued them highly and sometimes received tribute payments in the form of good-looking boys who were made into eunuchs to serve the court.[†]

The term translated "harem" in Esther 2:3 literally means "house of women." It consisted of special quarters in which the king's wives

---

exchange gifts, donate to charity, and eat a celebratory meal. At riotous celebrations, complete with noisemakers, people are sometimes encouraged to drink until they can no longer distinguish between the phrase "Blessed be Mordecai" and "Cursed be Haman."

[*] See Thomasino, "Esther," 3:480.

[†] Ibid., 3:478.

and concubines lived. Though taking more than one wife was practiced early in Israel's history, in later times only the king had concubines. In Persia and surrounding regions a man was allowed to have as many wives and concubines as he could afford. Though concubines held lesser status than wives, they were considered second wives. Though some concubines were free women from noble families, many were acquired as captives in war or as slaves. Usually chosen for their beauty, concubines often provided children in a childless marriage.*

Women like Esther who were candidates to replace Queen Vashti would have remained in the king's harem as wives or concubines regardless of whether they were chosen for the role. By fulfilling her duty as one of his many wives, Esther would not have been committing fornication when she slept with the king.

When Esther was elevated to the position of queen, she would have been installed in her own quarters apart from all the other women in the harem.

* Ibid., 3:484–485.

# THE TAKEAWAY

1. Scholars have noted that the word *God* is never used in the original Hebrew version of Esther's story, and yet it is evident that God's hand is on Esther. In what ways do you recognize God at work behind the scenes in Esther's story? In what ways, if any, do you recognize his behind-the-scenes work in your own life?

2. Psalm 27:14 urges us to

   Wait for the LORD;
      be strong and take heart
      and wait for the LORD.

   What evidence is there in Esther's story that she waited for the Lord? What do you think would have happened had she not?

3. How would you characterize your own experiences of waiting for the Lord? In what ways do you sense God may be inviting you to wait for him in this season of your life?

4. When she faced a difficult task, Esther fasted and asked others to fast on her behalf. Have you ever practiced the spiritual discipline of fasting? If so, what was the experience like?

5. During Purim, the Jewish people remind themselves that in every generation there will be people who will rise up to try to destroy them, just as Haman did. Why do you think they have been such frequent targets of persecution?

# CHAPTER 17

# A Wicked Outsider

## THE STORY OF THE WOMAN OF SAMARIA

### How a Loose Woman Becomes the First Evangelist

*But God hath chosen the foolish things of the world to confound the wise; and God hath chosen the weak things of the world to confound the things which are mighty; And base things of the world, and things which are despised, hath God chosen, yea, and things which are not, to bring to nought things that are.*

1 Corinthians 1:27 – 28

*F*ive hundred years is a long time to nurse a grudge. But the bitterness has been stoked and fed on both sides. As one rabbi liked to say, "Eating Samaritan food is like eating pig flesh."* An abomination. Filthy. Swinish. The Jews think of the Samaritans, who are a mixture of Jew and Gentile, as apostates and idol worshipers. The Samaritans are happy to return the favor.

Walking down the dusty path toward Jacob's Well is one of those half breeds, a woman who is familiar with condescension. More than once, she has felt the sting of holier-than-thou insults, often from neighbors, sometimes from Jews. Over the years, her heart has formed calluses to protect her from all the sneers and sideways glances. Even so, a rock of hurt—no, a block of ice—has managed to lodge itself inside her heart. It has been there so long she has nearly forgotten it. But she has not forgotten one thing. No matter the offense, there are always ways to retaliate.

As a young girl, she delighted in stories that gave the Jews the short end of the stick, like the one about a group of Samaritans who had strewn human bones in the Jerusalem temple one night. Their timing had been perfect. Defiling the Jewish holy place on the eve of Passover had prevented those high and mighty Jews from celebrating their precious feast that year.

As far as she knows, this enmity, this mutual hatred, between Samaritans and Jews has always been and always would be. But once Messiah came, everyone would know that it is the Samaritans and not the Jews who are Israel's true descendants and that Mount Gerizim is the one, true place of worship. After all, it was on this holy mountain

---

* I have paraphrased a quote, attributed to Rabbi Eliezer (c. AD 90–130), that read: "He that eats the bread of the Samaritans is like to one that eats the flesh of swine" (*m. Seb.* 8:10). Even though not a contemporary of the woman at the well, his attitude captures that of many of the Jews during the scene recounted in John's gospel.

that God's blessings were proclaimed when the tribes of Israel first passed into Canaan.

Drawing near the well of her forefather Jacob, which lies beneath the shadow of the holy mountain, she spots a stranger sitting on the thick capstone covering this deepest of wells. He is wearing *tefillin*, small, leather boxes attached to his forehead and his wrist that contain passages from Scripture in keeping with Moses' instructions regarding God's commands: "Tie them as symbols on your hands and bind them on your foreheads." A glance tells her he is Jewish. Beads of sweat glitter on his brow. It is the hottest part of the day.

Why is the man by himself? she wonders. He must be traveling north to Galilee, taking the shortcut that runs along the top of the ridge passing by Jacob's Well. She knows that many pious Jews avoid Samaria, claiming that even a tiny drop of saliva or a sip from a Samaritan cup will defile them. But this man seems neither worried nor hurried, only tired. And no wonder. It takes six hours to walk from Jerusalem to Mount Gerizim. But she is puzzled. What kind of traveler is he, lacking even a bucket made of skin — the type that can be unrolled and dipped into the well by ropes?* She doesn't know that his friends have taken it with them on their journey into town seeking provisions.

"Will you give me a drink?" the stranger startles her by breaking the silence, smiling as though to say he knows perfectly well he's crossing forbidden boundaries.

"Why do you ask me, a woman, for a drink?" she chides. "And why would a Jew even talk to a Samaritan?" Despite calling attention to his lack of manners, she flashes a quick smile, as though daring him to keep the conversation going.

She knows that any decent man will quickly withdraw at the sight of a solitary woman. But this man stays right where he is, and there is an appraising look in his eyes. A kind of hunger. She wonders what he really wants.

He is younger than she by several years. But what of it? Perhaps

---

* Though many translations depict the woman carrying a "water jar," Kenneth Bailey indicates that she was likely carrying a bucket made of skin, with crossed sticks at the top that kept the leather mouth open so it could be lowered into the well. Kenneth E. Bailey, *Jesus through Middle Eastern Eyes* (Downers Grove, IL: InterVarsity Press, 2008), 202.

he will be the adventure she is looking for. He speaks again, this time slowly with soft, enthralling words. "If you knew the gift of God and who it is that asks you for a drink, you would have asked him and he would have given you living water."

"But you have no bucket, and this well is deep," she says. "Where can you get this living water you talk about? Are you greater than Jacob, who gave us the well and drank from it himself, as did his sons and flocks and herds?"

Undeterred, he presses on, "Everyone who drinks this water will be thirsty again, but whoever drinks the water I give them will never thirst. Indeed, the water I give them will become in them a spring of water welling up to eternal life."

What kind of water can well up inside a person? "Then give me this water," she challenges, "so that I won't have to keep lugging a heavy bucket around in this intolerable heat."

There is no denying the heat. She has come by herself at midday, though women usually walk to the well in groups. They visit when it's coolest, drawing water in the early morning or a little before sunset. But this woman arrived alone at the most inhospitable time of day. What could it mean except that she is an outcast? That none of the village women want anything to do with her? That's why she braves the heat alone day after day. But she is not alone now.

"Go, call your husband and come back," the man says.

His words surprise her, cutting through her like a sickle slicing wheat. Why did he say that?

At a loss for how to deflect the question, she tells the truth. "I have no husband."

He presses her. "You are right when you say you have no husband. The fact is, you have had five husbands, and the man you now have is not your husband. What you have said is quite true."

His words are like arrows now, flying straight to her heart, piercing the ice that is lodged inside.

Attempting to ward him off, she tries a feint, hoping to start an argument. She's good at that.

Her arms are folded, her chin thrust forward. "Ah, I see you are a prophet," she says. "Tell me this, our fathers worshiped on Mount

Gerizim, but you Jews, you claim we must worship in Jerusalem." She waits for his angry retort, sure that it is coming.

But he will not fight with her. "Believe me," he says calmly, "the time is coming when you will worship the Father neither on this mountain nor in Jerusalem. You Samaritans worship what you do not know; we worship what we do know, for salvation is from the Jews. Yet a time is coming and has now come when the true worshipers will worship the Father in spirit and truth, for they are the kind of worshipers the Father seeks. God is spirit, and his worshipers must worship in spirit and truth."

Jewish to the core and yet he will not argue the preeminence of Jerusalem? Who is this man who thinks nothing of talking to Samaritans, who asks a woman for help, who even engages her in a theological conversation, and then goes on to read her heart? Even Samaritan men cannot do that.

This stranger seems to know everything about her, and yet he looks at her with so much love, as though she is treasured and cherished, as though it is the future and not the past that matters most.

She feels an absence of something familiar, a great weight being lifted from her. In his face, she sees neither condemnation nor rejection. Only an invitation.

"I know that Messiah is coming," she ventures. "When he comes, he will explain everything to us."

And then comes the spear thrust. "I who speak to you am he."

The ice that had frozen her heart and imprisoned her soul for so long begins to crack and melt, and a sense of peace invades her soul. She cannot keep the joy from her face.

Could this be the living water of which he speaks?

Before she has time to respond, she hears men approaching. "Rabbi," they hail him, "we found plenty of food in town. Figs and dates and bread and...." Their words trail off as they draw near. She can tell by the look on their faces that they are shocked to find their teacher* talking to a woman, especially to one like her.

Instead of facing them, she retreats, heading back into town. But this time it is not shame that hurries her feet away but excitement, a rush of

---

\* Rabbis did not generally speak to women, including their wives, in public.

wonder and delight. She can't wait to tell everyone about her encounter with the remarkable man who claims to be the Messiah.

"Come, see a man who told me everything I ever did. Could this be the Messiah?" she keeps telling everyone.

Women lay down their mending. Men put down their tools. A crowd gathers. What's that floozy up to now? Why is she so excited to tell them about a man who knows everything bad she's ever done? "This I've got to see," they say. And so they follow her.

Meanwhile, Jesus' disciples try to get him to eat something. Surely he must be as hungry as they are after their long journey.

But he denies it, says he's not the least bit hungry. "I have food to eat that you know nothing about."

"What? How could he possibly have found food?" they wonder. "Did somebody give him something to eat?"

"My food," Jesus explains to his disciples, "is to do the will of him who sent me and to finish his work."

Aware of the change that is already at work in the woman's heart, and knowing that many others will find him because of her, he continues, "Do you not say, 'Four months more and then the harvest?' I tell you, open your eyes and look at the fields! They are ripe for the harvest."

As he is speaking, the woman returns, hauling a crowd along with her. There, at the foot of their holy mountain, a group of Samaritans are blessed by the words of a Jewish rabbi. One by one, they welcome him into their hearts. They are so awestruck that they urge Jesus and his disciples to stay with them, and they do, for two more days.

Five hundred years of hostility begin to fall away because of his conversation with the woman at a well. No matter that the Jews destroyed the Samaritan temple on Mount Gerizim a hundred years before or that their people and his have always been enemies.

The Samaritans marvel at the love and power that emanates from him and at the words of hope he brings. "For God so loved the world," he tells them, "that he gave his one and only Son, that whoever believes in him shall not perish but have eternal life. For God did not send his Son into the world to condemn the world, but to save the world through him. Whoever believes in him is not condemned, but whoever does not believe stands condemned already because they have not believed in the name of God's one and only Son."

Just as they have always been told he would, the Messiah has come to them in the shadow of their sacred mountain. He is teaching them the way of salvation, restoring their dignity as men and women who have been specially chosen by God. Many believe, foremost among them the woman who had gone to the well by herself.

Living on the margins, shunned by her neighbors, she is no longer an outcast. She has a new life and friends—so many of them—brothers and sisters who also believe.

Amazing what one day can bring. She had gone to the well feeling forsaken and alone. But God had not forsaken her. Neither had he condemned her. Instead, he had seen the hurt in her heart and chosen her, a woman others had spurned, to be the first to preach the good news. No wonder that in her haste to tell the story, she left her water jar behind.*

## THE TIMES

Her story takes place sometime between the years AD 26 and 30.
*The Samaritan woman's story is found in John 4:1 – 42.*

Imagine a culture soaked in resentment, one that keeps a careful record of insults suffered at the hands of its near neighbor for hundreds of years. That's what Samaria was like in the early part of the first century. Perhaps it was not so unlike other regions of the country or other places in our world today.

Not quite Gentile and not quite Jewish, the Samaritans were descendants of Gentiles and Israelites, the latter of whom were left behind when many of their countrymen were taken into captivity in 722 BC, after the northern kingdom of Israel fell to Assyria.

Several hundred years later, in a failed attempt to improve relationships between Jews and Samaritans, Herod the Great married a Samaritan woman by the name of Malthrace, who became the mother of both Herod Antipas (the Herod who beheaded John the Baptist and

---

\* I am indebted to Kenneth E. Bailey for his insights into this story, which appear in his book *Jesus through Middle Eastern Eyes*, 200–216.

turned Jesus over to Pilate) and Herod Archelaus (the Herod who ruled Samaria, Judea, and Idumea from 4 BC to AD 6).

While the Jews considered the Samaritans impure, the Samaritans returned the compliment by calling the Jews apostates. The Samaritans accepted only the Pentateuch (the first five books of the Bible) in contrast to the entire Hebrew Scriptures, which encompassed the historical books and wisdom literature of the Bible. Instead of the temple in Jerusalem, they considered Mount Gerizim the one true place where God should be worshiped.

Built around the year 388 BC, their temple on the summit of Mount Gerizim endured for over 250 years until it was destroyed by the Jews in 128 BC. It is in the midst of such a hostile religious milieu that the story of the Samaritan woman unfolds. Remarkably, Jesus ignored the cultural markers of the day not only by speaking to a woman, but by speaking to a hated Samaritan with questionable morals.

Not only does Jesus ignore barriers of religion, race, and gender, but he chooses this setting in which to reveal himself for the first time as the Messiah. Perhaps Paul had this story in mind when he wrote to the church at Galatia, reminding them that "there is neither Jew nor Gentile, neither slave nor free, nor is there male and female, for you are all one in Christ Jesus" (Galatians 3:28).

# THE TAKEAWAY

1. What does Jesus' encounter with the Samaritan woman teach us about how to approach a stranger whose values and culture might be vastly different than our own?

2. This story speaks of water and harvest, of food and drink. At the beginning of the story, Jesus is hungry and thirsty. At the end he seems satisfied. Likewise, the woman has gone to the well because she needs water. But she returns to her village without her water jar. What do these interwoven themes of hunger, thirst, and harvest tell us about ourselves, about Jesus?

3. Some commentators suggest that the woman at the well may not have been as immoral as some have painted her.* Perhaps she did not divorce previous husbands, but they divorced her. Some of her husbands may have died. In such circumstances it wouldn't be surprising were she reduced to a life of poverty, forced to live with a man she wasn't married to simply as a way to survive. No matter what your take on the story, it would seem that she was both poor and marginalized. Yet Jesus took her seriously, engaged in a theological conversation with her, and then disclosed his identity as Messiah. He reached out to her with love and compassion, treating her with dignity. How has Christ reached out to you in the midst of your own hardships?

4. It is one thing to suffer hardship not of your own making and another to suffer the consequences of your own sinful choices. How have you experienced God's love despite your struggles with sin and imperfection?

5. Take a moment to pray through the story by imagining yourself as the woman at the well. As Jesus speaks to you, what are you thinking? How do you respond?

---

* See, for example, John Ortberg, *Who Is This Man? The Unpredictable Impact of the Inescapable Jesus* (Grand Rapids: Zondervan, 2012), 46–58.

# CHAPTER 18

# A Wicked Birthday Party

## THE STORY OF HERODIAS AND SALOME

### How a Wicked Mother-and-Daughter Combo Committed Bloody Murder

*And I saw the dead, small and great, stand before God; and the books were opened: and another book was opened, which is the book of life: and the dead were judged out of those things which were written in the books, according to their works.*

Revelation 20:12

*I*n the moonlight that streams through the window, she can see tiny beads of sweat glistening on his forehead. He is agitated and fitful, disturbed by some nocturnal vision. Even though she knows it's coming, she jumps when his scream tears the silence. And he jumps too, now wide awake. Herod Antipas sits up in bed, recalling the terror he's just lived through.

"It was John," he exclaims. "So real. I saw the slash across his neck, the blood streaming down his beard and clumping in his hair. Suddenly he appeared, out of the darkness, pointing straight at me. Though his mouth was closed, I heard him say: 'You viper! Even now the axe is laid to the root of the trees, and the trees that bear no fruit shall be cut down and cast into the fire.' He kept saying it, over and over, calling me a snake. I grabbed a club to beat him off, but he just stood there staring!

"Then I saw them, off to the side—a multitude of people screaming and in torment, burning but not burning up—and among them there was my face staring back at me!"

The tears are running down his face now. His body shakes. It has been like this off and on since the night of his birthday feast.

Herodias can still smell platters of meat, heaped high with sheep tail, roasted lamb, quail, and veal. She sees the servants weaving in and out of the raucous crowd, carrying trays loaded with grapes, figs, and dates, and delicate dishes made from gazelle meat and bird tongue. There are almonds, olives, pomegranates, and delicious desserts. High officials and military men have gathered to wish Herod well. Wearing garlands on their heads, the leading men of Galilee toast him with endless cups of wine imported from Italy and Cyprus. Paved in beautiful mosaic and bedecked with large, multicolored tapestries, the palace is filled with musicians, dancers, and storytellers whose only purpose is to amuse and delight.

The occasion is Herod's birthday. The location is Machaerus, a palatial stone fortress just east of the Dead Sea. Perched high upon a mountaintop, it is surrounded on three sides by deep ravines and boasts a commanding view of the eastern frontier. From its heights, Jerusalem and Jericho can plainly be seen. Like all fortresses, this one has its share of dungeons. Inside one of them, a man is fastened to the wall in chains. He is Herod's prisoner, a prophet named John.

A wild, unkempt man clad only in camel skin and a leather belt, John the Baptist both fascinates and repels Herod, who brings him out from time to time to hear him preach. The man is so compelling that Herod wonders what it might be like to follow him into the Jordan River so that John can baptize him. But how can he since John has already publicly condemned him, accusing him of committing incest by marrying Herodias, who was both his niece and his half-brother's wife?*

Still, Herod's sliver of a conscience tells him it would be a crime to kill a man as good as John. Plus, he fears that murdering the prophet will spark an insurrection. So instead of executing John as he might like to do, he lets him languish in prison for most of a year.

But Herodias will not let the matter drop. She despises John for condemning her divorce and remarriage and for doing it so publicly. How dare he threaten and thunder, dragging her name in the dirt, as though he is God? Whenever she speaks of him, Antipas catches a glint of malice in her eye that reminds him of his father of not so blessed memory.

Herod the Great was a man of grand ambitions and abilities. But he was grandly paranoid too. In addition to murdering several of his sons, he put all the baby boys of Bethlehem to death merely on talk of a star and a little child destined to be king. Caesar Augustus once joked that he would rather be Herod's pig (*hus*) than his son (*huis*), because as a nominal Jew, Herod would at least have had some scruples about slaughtering a pig, though he certainly had none about executing members of his own family.

Herodias herself is the granddaughter of Herod the Great and therefore her husband's niece. Living in the shadow of her grandfather's

---

* The Jews would have considered Herod's marriage to his niece, who was also his half-brother's wife, to be incestuous (see Leviticus 18:16 and 20:21).

monstrous paranoia, she is aware that her own father, grandmother, and several of her uncles were among his many victims. With ten wives, he had plenty of children to fear. But Herodias was not one of them. Instead, she was numbered among his favorite grandchildren. Doting on her, he arranged a marriage with one of his surviving sons, her uncle Herod Philip.

But Philip was landless and crownless, and if Herodias longed for anything, it was for a glittering crown to wear on her head. While she was thinking of how to acquire one, Philip's half-brother Antipas happened to visit them at their home in Rome. He stayed for days and days and was so smitten by Herodias that he begged her to leave Philip and marry him. Herodias was shameless and clever and would not abandon her husband unless Antipas promised to divorce his wife, a Nabatean princess, who was the daughter of King Aretas IV.

So Herod Antipas destroyed his alliance with Aretas by divorcing his wife, and Herodias abandoned her current uncle-husband to acquire another.

Though she loves him, Herodias thinks Herod Antipas is something of a disappointment. Merely a tetrarch, who rules Galilee and Perea—the land beyond the Jordan—he has not yet managed to grace her brow with a crown. As it happens, Antipas's territory is the region in which both John and his cousin Jesus can most frequently be found, preaching, teaching, performing wonders, and stirring up trouble.

Like all the Herods, Herodias is a schemer. But her first scheme, to use Herod Antipas as a stepping stone to power, had been openly challenged by John, whose insolence quickly ignited her wrath. So she decided to silence him, if not all at once then in measured steps. She began by pressuring Herod to imprison the popular prophet. Once John was thrown into jail, she waited for an opportune time to finish him off. She pressured Herod, but without results. How is it, she wondered, that even though she is only a woman, she is twice the man her husband is?

Then comes Herod's birthday celebration, the perfect occasion to complete her scheme. She relies on Salome, the daughter she bore to her first husband, Herod Philip. Dressing her in a costume of glittering silver, she instructs her daughter to perform her most beguiling dance. Herodias has carefully calculated the moment, counting on Salome's performance to create the perfect climax for her husband's boisterous birthday party. And she is not disappointed.

With a sultry smile, Salome spins and twirls, extending her arms in a great, expanding circle as she moves across the floor, inviting every man to imagine what it would be like to become her intimate acquaintance. Finally, when she has exhausted every seductive surprise, she comes to rest like a delicate bouquet at Herod's feet.

"Bravo!" he says, and all his guests rise to applaud her.

"Ask me for whatever you want and I'll give it, up to half my kingdom!" he declares.

Excusing herself for just one moment, Salome hurries out to consult her mother. "Ask him," Herodias whispers, "for the head of John the Baptist."

Returning at once, the young girl appears before Herod and says, "I want you to give me right now the head of John the Baptist on a platter."

The request dismays Herod. He had not seen this coming. The political climate is not conducive for executing such a man. Plus it is a violation of the law to carry out a sentence or to behead a man without first holding a trial. But he has made a public oath and will not shame himself by rescinding it in front of so many powerful men. Immediately he orders John's execution.

In a few minutes 'time, while the guests are still murmuring about Salome's extraordinary dance and her shocking request, the executioner returns. He is holding a large platter on which John's head rests. He presents it to Salome, who then presents it to her mother, who accepts it with great pleasure.

On hearing of John's murder, his disciples come and take his body and lay it gently in a tomb.

When Jesus learns of his cousin's death, he withdraws from the ever-present crowd to be alone and pray. Grieving for John, the best man he has ever known, his own future comes clearly into view.

As the fame of Jesus spreads, people begin to say that he is John the Baptist risen from the dead. Even Herod is haunted by the possibility and has been overheard, saying, "John, the man I beheaded, has been raised from the dead."

Herodias believes no such nonsense and is haunted by nothing but her continued ambition to one day become a queen. But there is more horror to come. In due time, she will accompany Herod to Jerusalem for the Feast of Passover. She will be present on the day that Jesus, the one they call the Christ, appears before him accused of many crimes.[*]

Later, after John and Jesus have both been executed, one by Herod and the other by Pontius Pilate, now Herod's bosom friend, she will watch her husband's armies flee from King Aretas, who is determined to avenge himself on the man who years earlier had divorced his daughter to marry someone else.

Herod Antipas is so thoroughly defeated that many think of his humiliation as divine retribution for beheading John. Still, Herodias pursues her schemes of greatness, this time urging Herod Antipas to go to Rome in order to petition Emperor Caligula to bestow on him a royal crown. But her brother Agrippa is a clever liar who sends a messenger ahead of them accusing Herod of sedition. Stripping him of all his lands and goods, Caligula banishes Herod and Herodias to Gaul, where Herod soon perishes.

Though Herodias lives on, her story fades. We don't know what becomes of her. Whether her calloused heart led her into yet more wicked schemes or whether it was softened by the loss of everything she ever wanted, we will never know. What we do know is that she was guilty of at least one great act of wickedness, choosing to murder the man who through his powerful preaching turned the hearts of many wayward people back to the God who loved them.

## THE TIMES

Her story takes place between AD 27 and 29
*Herodias and Salome's story can be found in Matthew*
*14:3 – 12; Mark 6:14 – 29; Luke 3:19 – 20; 9:7 – 9.*

Herodias's grandfather, Herod the Great, became military governor of Galilee in 47 BC when he was only twenty-five years old. Seven years later, the Roman Senate appointed him king of Judea. When Herod

---

[*] Though the gospel does not say this, it is a reasonable assumption that Herodias would have traveled to Jerusalem with her husband at that time.

became king, he embarked on massive building projects, including the expansion of the temple in Jerusalem and the construction of the port city of Caesarea Maritima.

Alerted by Magi from the east about a child in Bethlehem who was destined to become king of the Jews, he massacred every boy under the age of two in order to prevent the rise of a contender. He ruled until 4 BC, when according to the Jewish historian Josephus, he died an excruciating death, his body filled with worms. Prior to his death, Herod, who was half Jewish, ordered the leading Jews in the area to a stadium in Jericho where they were then held prisoner. Knowing his own people hated him, he gave orders for his soldiers to execute the leaders at the moment of his death so that there would be universal mourning when he passed. Fortunately his order was never carried out.

After his death, Herod the Great's territory was divided among three of his sons: Archelaus, Philip,* and his youngest son, Antipas. Archelaus proved to be a cruel and incompetent leader. He was banished by the Roman emperor Caligula, and Judea was made a Roman province, which was then governed by a series of prefects, the best known of whom is Pontius Pilate.

From the evidence presented in the gospels, it appears that Herod was fascinated by both John the Baptist and Jesus. Since his estates were managed by a man named Cuza, whose wife Joanna was a disciple of Jesus, it is possible that Cuza and Joanna spoke to Herod and Herodias about Jesus.

A group of Pharisees warned Jesus that Herod intended to kill him. Jesus responded by saying, "Go tell that fox, 'I will keep on driving out demons and healing people today and tomorrow, and on the third day I will reach my goal.' In any case, I must press on today and tomorrow and the next day—for surely no prophet can die outside Jerusalem!"

Herod was hoping to see Jesus face to face so that he could witness his wonders firsthand. The two finally met when Pilate learned that Herod was in Jerusalem for Passover. As a Galilean, Jesus was under Herod's jurisdiction. When Herod ridiculed and mocked Jesus and then released him to Pilate since he could find no reason to charge him, the two former enemies became friends (Luke 23:6–12).

---

* Not Herodias's first husband Herod Philip but Philip the tetrarch, who later married Salome, the daughter of Herodias.

Throughout his rule, Herod Antipas was reviled by his Jewish subjects. As an Idumean, whose family descended from Esau rather than Jacob, and as a Samaritan on his mother's side, he was never trusted by the people he governed.

## THE TAKEAWAY

1. Both Herod and Herodias would have had some exposure to John's preaching with its emphasis on repentance. He may even have spoken to them about Jesus. What has been your own experience of the connection between repentance and new life?

2. What might have prevented Herodias from turning toward God and away from her sins? What prevents you from doing the same?

3. Why is power often such a corrupting force even among good people? How have you handled power, whether on a large or small scale, in your own life?

4. Has God ever called you to speak uncomfortable truths to people of influence? How did you respond? How did they respond?

5. How do you respond when someone criticizes you?

# CHAPTER 19

# *Wicked Tears*

## THE STORY OF THE WOMAN WHO WIPED THE FEET OF JESUS

### How a Prostitute Lets Down Her Hair, Scandalizing Everyone but Jesus

*Blessed are ye, when men shall hate you, and when they shall separate you from their company, and shall reproach you, and cast out your name as evil, for the Son of man's sake.*

Luke 6:22

$\mathcal{S}$he sits on the floor with a handful of others, beggars mostly. Unlike the dull-colored robes that help them blend into the wall they lean against, her woven red cloak demands attention. Her hair is swept upward, under a gold-colored head covering, revealing a well-shaped face. Dark eyes find their complement in full, red lips that seem on the verge of smiling.

Yet Simon passes by her without allowing himself the luxury of a sideways glance. Tonight he has thrown open his doors to one and all, even to women like her. Anyone who wants supper can have it as long as he or she agrees to wait until the honored guests have finished their meal. It is the usual custom, a way to seek God's blessing and display one's generosity to the less fortunate. So they wait—silently, politely, willing their stomachs to be quiet lest they disturb the banquet that will soon commence.

She is glad to be among them, though it's not the feast that has drawn her. In her lap she holds an alabaster jar filled with expensive perfume. She is waiting for someone.

Simon surveys the room, his glance resting not on the riffraff leaning against the wall but on several broad couches arranged in the shape of a U that will provide a comfortable place for his guests to recline and enjoy their leisurely meal. A table filled with figs, fish, grapes, bread, olives, dates, and roasted goat meat will be set in place once every man has taken his place.

He knows that most of his guests will be eager, as he is, to examine the controversial young rabbi, the one they call Jesus. Many of Simon's fellow Pharisees have their doubts about the man. For one thing, he consorts with tax collectors who are merely Roman stooges disguised as Jews. These men grow fat by squeezing money from their own people, taking their cut and then passing the rest on to the Romans. For another, his disciples seem crude and uneducated, rough fishermen who are always eating and drinking but never fasting. They have even been spotted picking grain and eating it on the Sabbath. And why, when there are six days a week to work, would Jesus choose to desecrate the seventh day by healing a man with a withered arm as he had recently done?

Still, Jesus attracts ever larger crowds, drawing from the unschooled masses, who are always clamoring for the next miracle. His following has grown so quickly that certain Pharisees have come from Jerusalem for a closer look. Simon has spoken to these men. He knows their concerns.

Lately, another sensational story has been making the rounds. A few days ago, they say, Jesus healed a paralyzed man who was lowered through a rooftop into his presence. Simon has no problem with the idea that a sage could possess healing powers. But Jesus had the audacity to tell the man his sins were forgiven — an obvious blasphemy since only God can forgive sin.

Simon has invited the rabbi to his home to see for himself, to test him and discover just what he is made of. Perhaps the tales people tell of him are not all true. Jesus is young. There may still be time to turn him to the right way.

As is customary, Simon honors his guests by welcoming each with a kiss. He provides water for washing the dust from their feet and olive oil to serve as soap for their hands and anointing oil for their heads.

But what of Jesus? How will Simon greet this popular rabbi when he arrives? Hosting a sage is considered a great honor. But what if the rabbi's teachings are suspect? Simon has thought long and hard about this and has decided that too warm a welcome could be misconstrued. His other guests might draw the wrong conclusions.

Meanwhile, the young woman continues to wait, sitting quietly in the corner of the room. Simon seems oblivious to her presence. But she notices everything and everyone. To pass the time, her mind drifts back to her first encounter with the rabbi. She was one among hundreds, eager to see him perform wonders and hear him preach. In the midst of the enormous crowd, it seemed to her as though he were speaking only to her.

"Blessed are you who are poor,
  for yours is the kingdom of God.

Blessed are you who hunger now,
   for you will be satisfied.
Blessed are you who weep now,
   for you will laugh.
Blessed are you when people hate you,
   when they exclude you and insult you
   and reject your name as evil,
     because of the Son of Man."

"Do not judge, and you will not be judged. Do not condemn, and you will not be condemned. Forgive, and you will be forgiven."

The wind carries his voice to her across the crowd. His words fall strong and clear and straight into her soul. She begins to pray aloud as many others in the crowd are doing, tears streaming down their faces.

What is this she feels, this warm, enfolding presence? It is the Shekinah* of God that has descended on her and many others. No longer afraid to face and name her sins, she brings them to mind one by one and then leaves them in the hands of God. There is so much she has to admit and surrender. Rebellion, hurt, rage, unfaithfulness.

Names pass her lips as well, and she sees the faces of the men who paid to sleep with her. They are legion. In this sacred moment she finds the strength to give each man into God's own hands. She has been the object of their lust, and now they will be the object of God's mercy. As she forgives each one, a knot of worthlessness unties itself inside her and is replaced with a sense of peace and freedom.

She hears the words of Jesus again, "But love your enemies, do good to them, and lend to them without expecting to get anything back. Then your reward will be great, and you will be children of the Most High, because he is kind to the ungrateful and wicked. Be merciful, just as your Father is merciful."

That God loves sinners, this is the message that has drawn her, a wonder that has altered her life. She had hardly imagined that God would do anything but despise her. That he could cherish her and call her his own, this upends her world.

---

* *Shekinah* is a Hebrew word that refers to the experienced presence of God dwelling with his people. While it is not a word that occurs in the Bible, the Jews used it to designate the presence of God in Israel's history.

Her thoughts are interrupted by Jesus' arrival at Simon's house. Now there is no crowd separating them, only a small group of men who are talking with Simon. She watches as he walks into the room. To her surprise, there is no amiable welcome—no kiss, no water for his feet, no oil for his head. Simon merely nods in acknowledgment of his guest and then turns his back, continuing to converse with others.

The insult is obvious. She feels the sudden tension that has entered the room. Everyone expects the young rabbi to react, to explode perhaps, to shake the dust from his feet and leave the Pharisee's house. What will he do?

She is used to snubs from men like Simon. Even men who pay for the privilege of abusing her body maintain the pretense of a righteous life by keeping their distance in public places. But she has never seen such treatment of a rabbi. Hospitality has always been a sacred trust. To treat a guest this way brings shame.

She feels it strongly, as though Jesus has just been slapped in the face and the pain has radiated across the room and landed on her cheek. Her face flushes from the insult.

But Jesus shows no sign of anger. Instead of turning his back on the gathering as one might expect, he merely walks over to a couch and reclines, waiting for the meal to begin. But this in itself is shocking. For it is always the eldest and wisest who reclines first while the rest of the guests take their places in order of seniority. As one of the youngest men in the room, Jesus has just made a remarkable statement.

Missing nothing of what is happening, the woman leaves her place near the wall, infuriated by how her beloved rabbi is being treated. She had intended to anoint his hands and head with perfume as a way of thanking him for his gift of forgiveness. But since he is already reclining, she can only reach his feet. Sensing the rejection he must feel, she kneels before him and begins to weep, and then she does the unthinkable. Uncovering her head, she unwinds long, dark strands of hair, using them to wipe the flood of tears that have fallen on his feet. Kissing his feet, she anoints them with the perfume. With this dramatic gesture, too intimate for public display, she shares his humiliation and performs a service his host has deliberately withheld.

"Disgusting!" Simon thinks. "Clearly, my concerns regarding the rabbi are well founded." For he knows that no self-respecting woman would show her hair to her husband until their wedding night. Simon sees her gesture as a declaration of intimacy.

"If he were a prophet," Simon thinks, "he would know who is touching him and what kind of woman she is—that she is a sinner." But instead of rebuking her, Jesus appears to welcome the attention.

"Simon," Jesus says, as though reading his thoughts, "I have something to tell you."

"Tell me, teacher," he replies.

"Two people owed money to a certain moneylender. One owed him five hundred denarii, and the other fifty. Neither of them had the money to pay him back, so he forgave the debts of both. Now which of them will love him more?"

Simon knows that five hundred denarii is a lot of money—two years' wages for a laborer while fifty denarii represents only two months' worth of wages—so he makes the expected reply: "I suppose the one who had the bigger debt forgiven."

"You have judged correctly," Jesus says. And by his tone, Simon catches a hint that the rabbi is also inferring that Simon has not always judged correctly.

Turning toward the woman who has exposed herself to ridicule for his sake, Jesus continues. "Do you see this woman, Simon?"

The question forces Simon to look at the woman, to see her for the first time.

"I came into your house," Jesus continues. "You did not give me any water for my feet, but she wet my feet with her tears and wiped them with her hair. You did not give me a kiss, but this woman, from the time I entered, has not stopped kissing my feet. You did not put oil on my head, but she has poured perfume on my feet. Therefore, I tell you, her many sins have been forgiven—as her great love has shown. But whoever has been forgiven little loves little."

Then Jesus turns his attention to the woman, who is still kneeling before him. "Your sins," he says, "are forgiven....Your faith has saved you; go in peace." And she does.

The guests begin to murmur, saying to each other, "Who is this who even forgives sins?"

Afterward, Simon wonders the same. Though he tells himself he is in the right, he feels confused. His lips begin to tremble slightly. He feels off kilter. A small tear runs down his cheek. Working hard to put the matter from his mind, he can't quite manage it, can't stop asking himself, "Who is this man who offers to forgive my sins?"*

## THE TIMES

Her story takes place sometime between the years AD 26 and 30.
*This woman's story is told in Luke 7:36–50.*

In the Middle East, hospitality has always been considered a sacred responsibility. To refrain from caring for guests would have been considered a grievous offense.

Mealtimes were often leisurely, especially if guests were being entertained. To eat with someone meant that you enjoyed a good relationship, that there was peace between you, which is why so many religious people were scandalized by the meals Jesus shared with notorious sinners.

Instead of sitting down at a table as we do today, people either sat on mats on the floor or reclined on couches. At least one scholar† thinks that Jesus and his disciples were reclining on mats or cushions on the floor rather than on elevated couches when they ate their last meal together before his death. For formal dinners, guests sometimes reclined on a *triclinium,* a seating area made up of couches arranged in the form of a U. The food would be served on a removable platter that served as the tabletop for a three-legged table. Rather than using silverware, people simply tore off a piece of bread and used it to scoop food from a common bowl.

It was the host's responsibility not only to care for his guests but to protect them from harm, even to the point of defending them with his life should that be necessary.

---

* I am indebted to Kenneth E. Bailey for his fascinating interpretation of this story in his book *Jesus through Middle Eastern Eyes* (Downers Grove, IL: InterVarsity Press, 2008), 239–60. Though Bailey does not speculate on whether Simon showed signs of repentance as I have done in this story, he does make it clear that the story Jesus tells Simon speaks of forgiveness that is extended to both people, the one with the large debt and the one with the small one, implying that Simon is the person with the smaller debt.

† Dr. Steven Notley as mentioned in Ann Spangler and Lois Tverberg, *Sitting at the Feet of Rabbi Jesus* (Grand Rapids: Zondervan, 2009), 204.

With this as the backdrop, we can see the story more clearly. Not only did Simon refrain from offering the usual kiss as Jesus entered his home, but he withheld common courtesies, like providing water and olive oil for Jesus to wash his hands and feet. By not offering these amenities, especially to a rabbi, Simon delivered a stinging, public insult.

But what was a prostitute doing at the house of a Pharisee, a man who would have considered her unfit for his table? To show one's magnanimity, it was common practice to invite outcasts to a formal meal. But these unfortunates were only allowed to eat once all the other guests had completed the meal. Rather than crashing the party, this woman may have humbled herself by identifying with outcasts, thus exposing herself to ridicule because of her desire to thank Jesus for everything he'd done for her.

# THE TAKEAWAY

1. Comment on the role reversal that takes place in this story with a "law breaker" becoming the hero while a "law keeper" seems to be the villain.

2. What does this woman's story say about the human tendency to judge others by outward appearances? How have you experienced this tendency in your own life, either in judging others or sensing their judgment against you?

3. As you think about the story, take a moment to consider which of the characters you identify with the most. Are you a beggar leaning against the wall and watching the scene unfold, the host who is trying to put the young rabbi in his place, one of the guests, or the woman herself? What makes you identify with that person?

4. Have you ever loved someone so much that you didn't care what other people thought? What might your relationship with Christ look like if you loved him that much?

5. This story highlights the fact that faith is not merely something we *think* but something we *do*. Briefly share about an experience that enabled you to express your faith through action. In what ways, if any, did your behavior put you at risk of disapproval from others (as the woman did when she washed Jesus' feet with her tears)?

6. Jesus says those who've been forgiven much love much. Take a moment to consider whether there are sins you haven't yet admitted, perhaps even to yourself. Let this woman's story encourage you to tell God everything that is in your heart.

# CHAPTER 20

# *Wicked Crazy*

## THE STORY OF MARY MAGDALENE

### How a Demon-Possessed Woman
### Becomes a Devoted Disciple

*And they brought unto him all sick people that were taken
with divers diseases and torments, and those which were
possessed with devils, and those which were lunatick, and
those that had the palsy; and he healed them.*

Matthew 4:24

*H*e is close enough to smell her unwashed body and to see the caked-on dirt that lines her fingernails. Greasy strands of hair straggle from beneath her scarf, framing a face that looks far older than it is. She is sitting in shadows, rocking back and forth and looking straight through him, as though he doesn't exist. He watches as she clutches her throat, vainly trying to throttle the voices that come unbidden.

Her fits arrive like sudden tempests. Gales of shrieking laughter, followed by loud wailing, and then a long spell of muttering, as though she is conversing with ghosts that no one else can see. He listens to their changing pitch as one follows another in quick succession. One is low and threatening, the next high and wheedling. They snarl, quarrel, and bite each other, this tangle of demons that lives inside her.

The town of Magdala is used to Mary's fits. She is mad, they say, hopeless and beyond help. Surely she has committed terrible sins to deserve such torment. Unable to comprehend her, people simply ignore her. All except the children, who cringe and keep their distance. The mean ones taunt her, calling out "Devil Girl!" or "Witch!" whenever she passes by.

But she is no witch. Only a tortured soul whose mind has already descended into hell while her body lives on earth.

Jesus knows this. That's why he's come to save her. As he steps closer, she grabs a fistful of stones from the mound of small rocks heaped beside her feet. Before she can launch the first, she hears him saying something sharp and clear: "Come out!"

His voice is so commanding that it shakes her to the core. She feels the ground begin to roll and quake. But instead of swallowing her whole and dragging her down to the grave, as she thinks it must, it shatters something deep inside, a locked place filled with fear. Then, with a shudder, she feels them leave. Before she can make sense of what has happened, she hears screams of mingled rage and terror. Disembodied now, the demons howl and fade away.

A great weight of anguish has been lifted, and she is herself again. How long has she been trapped beneath the darkness that took possession of her soul? She cannot say. She only knows her chains are broken. She feels so light she thinks she will float away.

"Mary," Jesus says, calling her to himself. His voice is tender now, as though he has known her all her life. When she takes his outstretched hands in hers, she sees in his expression only love and mercy, but so deep and wide she cannot measure it. Tears roll softly down her cheeks, and a smile lights her face—the first in many years.

Months later, she has become a kind of celebrity. "There she is!" People point and jostle for a closer look as a group of Jesus' disciples pass by. They cannot imagine how such a stately woman, tall and self-possessed, could have been lost in so much darkness. But many have heard the story from eyewitnesses, friends and family members who were present when the miracle occurred.

Now Mary of Magdala travels freely with those who number themselves among Jesus' close disciples. Joanna, Susanna, and several other female disciples pay for Jesus' expenses out of their own purses.[*] Wherever they go, they are the topic of conversation. To see a band of men and women roaming from town to town as they follow their rabbi is surprising if not shocking, a matter of outrage to some[†] who see it as yet another mark against this controversial rabbi. For women normally travel in the company of unrelated men only when they are able to spend the night with relatives.

But Mary cares nothing for convention or about where she will rest her head at night. She simply wants to be with Jesus. To love and serve him and to learn from him and follow him. So she is there on the mountaintop when he multiplies bread to feed thousands and there when he astonishes the poor and the rich by declaring that the first will

---

[*] That Jesus had female disciples is attested to in Matthew 12:48–50; Luke 8:1–3; 10:38; and Acts 9:36.

[†] Though the gospels don't comment on whether anyone was scandalized by the fact that female disciples traveled with Jesus and his male disciples, it is likely that the social scene presented in the gospel would have been extraordinary. See Kenneth E. Bailey, *Jesus through Middle Eastern Eyes* (Downers Grove, IL: InterVarsity Press, 2008), 192–93.

be last and the last will be first. She watches as he opens the eyes of the blind and enables the lame to walk. Whenever Jesus drives out demons, she is the first to share her story and pray with those who've been set free. A leader among the women, she buoys everyone by her faith.

Mary has been traveling the length and breadth of Galilee and Judea with Jesus and the other disciples. Now they are heading into Jerusalem for the feast of Passover. The city has become a cauldron of political and religious fervor. Accompanied by a great crush of people, they walk down the Mount of Olives beside Jesus who is riding a donkey—a symbol of humility, indicating that he will ascend his throne through peaceful rather than violent means. Voices in the crowd acclaim him, shouting:

"Hosanna to the Son of David!"

"Blessed is he who comes in the name of the Lord!"

"Hosanna in the highest heaven."

Mary feels a thrill at his triumphant entry into the city, as he rides over the cloaks and palm branches people have strewn across the road. Despite the fact that he has encountered stubborn opposition from the religious elite, ordinary people acclaim him as Israel's long-desired king. She wonders what the next few days will hold and what wondrous work God will do to put Jesus on the throne.

Though Mary is aware of the political risks, she is certain that nothing is impossible for God. Haven't the prophets spoken of this day? Hasn't God provided miracles and wonders pointing to the fact that Jesus is the Messiah they've all been waiting for?

In the midst of her jubilation, Mary cannot imagine that in just a few days she will become part of another crowd, a great throng of people who will accompany Jesus again. But this time he will be on his way out of the city and up to the place of execution.

Joining thousands of other pilgrims, Mary stays in Jerusalem to celebrate the great feast of Passover. Like the rest of her people, she will commemorate God's deliverance by recalling the wonderful deeds he did for them in Egypt, delivering them from the hand of their oppressors and leading them to the land of promise. It is a time of feasting and celebration that will last late into the night.

When Mary finally awakens it is not to rumors of glory but to unthinkable disaster. She hears that the Lord has been arrested, tried, whipped, and sentenced to death! Even now he is being marched to the quarry* outside the city walls† where criminals are crucified.

She hurries to join the swelling crowd, hoping the rumors are false. As she makes her way through the mob she looks for Jesus' disciples. But most are nowhere to be seen.‡ Then she catches sight of her friends — Mary the mother of Jesus, Salome, and Mary the mother of James and Joseph. They are clinging to each other, inconsolable. Jesus is lying on the ground a few feet from them. A heavy beam has fallen across his shoulders, and his tunic is soaked in blood. On his head he wears a crown of thorns.

"Get up, king!" the soldiers yell, grabbing his arm and pulling him to his feet. As Jesus staggers forward, the women try to break through the crowd to reach him. But the soldiers push them back, and the women's anguished cries are drowned by the deafening roar of the mob.

Now Mary is holding on to Salome's hand as the two stumble forward, toward the place of crucifixion. She watches as Jesus is stripped§ and nailed to the crossbeam, which is then fastened to a tall upright beam that's already fixed in the ground.¶ Soldiers press his legs to either side of the wood, driving long nails into his ankles in order to fasten him to the cross.**

The scene is so gruesome that many who witness it double over, unable to control their nausea. Though Mary has seen countless cruci-fied men lining the road before, she has never been this close. Unwilling

---

* The gospels indicate that Jesus was crucified at Golgotha, or "the place of the skull." Though we don't know its exact location, the Church of the Holy Sepulchre, which was built in the fourth century, marks the likely spot today. At the time of Jesus, this may have been an oval-shaped abandoned quarry where there were both tombs and gardens. See David E. Garland, "Mark," *Zondervan Illustrated Bible Backgrounds Commentary*, ed. Clinton E. Arnold (Grand Rapids: Zondervan, 2002), 1:298–99.

† Both Roman and Jewish law mandated that crucifixions take place outside the city walls. The Romans usually planted crosses along heavily trafficked roads so that this gruesome form of execution would serve as a deterrent to would-be criminals and rabble rousers.

‡ John's gospel is the only one of the four gospels to indicate that any of Jesus' twelve disciples were present. See John 19:27.

§ Though victims were often crucified without clothing, the Romans were aware of Jewish scruples about nakedness and would probably have left Jesus with a loincloth. See David E. Garland, "Mark," 1:301.

¶ Wood was scarce, so crossbeams may have been used more than once. They were carried by the condemned person to the place of execution and then affixed to upright beams or trees that were already in place.

** Crosses could be shaped like an X, Y, I, or T. See note on John 19:17, *Archaeological Study Bible*, ed. Walter C. Kaiser Jr. (Grand Rapids: Zondervan, 2005), 1758.

to spare herself the pain her Lord endures, she faces forward along with the other women who keep vigil, watching and waiting. As people pass in and out of the city along the busy road that skirts the quarry, some stop and shake their heads, mocking Jesus. "You who are going to destroy the temple and build it in three days, save yourself! Come down from the cross, if you are the Son of God." And then they laugh.

The priests and the elders laugh too, saying, "He saved others, but he can't save himself! He trusts in God, let God rescue him."

Mary wants to slap them, to scream in their faces and tell them the truth, that of all the fools who ever walked upon the earth they are the worst. But before she can make a move, darkness descends over the entire area, covering everything. Her heart feels the weight of a sorrow too deep to voice. Despite the burden of her grief, she will not leave. How can she abandon her deliverer when there is no one to deliver him?

After a long while, she hears Jesus crying out in a loud voice, *"Eli, Eli, lema sabachthani?"* (which means, "My God, my God, why have you forsaken me?").

She feels it now, the agony she tried to keep her heart from knowing. The question she cannot stop herself from asking breaks out: "Where is Abba? How can he abandon his beloved Son to the torment of the cross?"

Through the shadows she sees men moving. They are lifting up a sponge soaked in wine and fastened to a stick, offering it to Jesus. Then she hears Jesus cry out again in a loud voice, saying, "Father, into your hands I commit my spirit." His head slumps forward onto his chest as he draws his last breath.

Before Mary and the other women can voice their grief, the earth begins to shake and rumble. Huge rocks split apart. Crevices open in the earth. Those who had been mocking Jesus a few moments earlier now cower in the darkness that surrounds them.

When the earth finally settles, they slink away, one by one. Now only the women are left, along with a few Roman soldiers who stay behind to guard the body. By evening, a secret disciple of Jesus, a wealthy man by the name of Joseph of Arimathea, arrives. He has obtained permission to remove the broken body from the cross and carry it to a tomb that's been freshly carved in a section of the quarry. As Mary watches, she is grateful that at least Jesus will not suffer the disgrace of a shameful burial, his body flung into a common pit along with executed criminals.

Sitting opposite the tomb, Mary watches as Jesus is carefully laid to rest. Loaded down with spices,* Joseph and Nicodemus, a member of the Jewish ruling council and a secret follower of Jesus, crouch low to enter the tomb. Packing the body, they wrap it in linen strips as is the custom. Once they finish, they seal the tomb by rolling a large stone across the entrance, preventing animals from entering.

That night Mary barely sleeps. Passing in and out of dreams, she listens as the shrill voices of her old tormenters batter her heart. Taunting and triumphant, they tell her they have won and that they will soon return and never leave. No one can help her now.

But the love of God creates a barrier they cannot pass.

On Sunday, Mary rises, early, before daybreak, and hurries to Jesus' grave along with two other women — Salome and Mary the mother of James. It is the only thing she can think to do. She and the other women carry spices they will use to anoint his body. Leaving soon after sunrise, they remember the large stone that bars the entryway to the tomb. Who will roll it away so they can enter?

But there is no need to worry, because the stone has already been rolled away. Peering inside, Mary realizes that Jesus' body is gone. Someone has stolen it! Rushing into the city, she finds Peter and John, telling them, "They've taken the Lord and we don't know where they've put him!"

Running to the grave, Peter enters first. He sees strips of linen lying on the ground and the burial cloth that had been around Jesus' head now neatly folded and set aside.

After the two men return to the city, Mary remains at the tomb, weeping. Bending over to look inside, she is startled by two angels in brilliant white, seated on the ledge where Jesus' body had been.

"Woman, why are you crying?" they ask.

"They've taken my Lord away, and I don't know where they've put him."

---

* John 19:39 indicates that Nicodemus brought with him about seventy-five pounds of myrrh and aloes, an astonishing amount in line with what would have been used for royal burials. See note on John 19:39, *Archaeological Study Bible*, 1760.

Then from behind her, another voice inquires: "Why are you weeping? Who is it you are looking for?"

Turning around she sees a man she thinks must be the gardener. Pleading with him, she says, "Sir, if you have carried him away, tell me where you have put him, and I will get him." Though Mary had been powerless to prevent Jesus' shameful death, she will do anything to ensure he is treated reverently in death.

Then a single word disarms her. "Mary," the man says, and the tenderness in his voice is unmistakable.

"Rabboni!" she exclaims.

Before she can reach out and touch him, Jesus says, "Do not hold on to me, for I have not yet returned to the Father. Go instead to my brothers and tell them, 'I am returning to my Father and your Father, to my God and your God.'"

Suddenly the darkness that has been stalking Mary for the last three days lifts and an explosion of joy fills her soul. Jesus is alive! Death has been defeated! Anything is possible now!

So Mary Magdalene, from whom Jesus had expelled seven demons, is chosen by God to be present at the moment the greatest story in the history of the world reaches its stunning climax. Loving Jesus to the bitterest of bitter ends, she is the first person to be given the honor of sharing the good news of his resurrection from the dead, telling others, "I have seen the Lord!"

## THE TIMES

Her story probably took place between AD 27 and 30.
Mary Magdalene's story is told in Matthew 27:56, 61; Mark 15:40,
47; 16:1 – 11; Luke 8:2; 24:10; John 19:25; 20:1 – 18.

In the ancient Near East, belief in demons and in the power of magical incantations and amulets to control them was common. By contrast, the Bible discouraged people from the use of magic or from trying to make contact with spirits. Both the Old and New Testaments make it clear that only God has complete power over evil spirits. Notably, when Jesus delivered Mary and others from evil spirits, he did so based on his authority and not on the use of magical incantations or objects.

Throughout the centuries, many writers have mistakenly portrayed Mary Magdalene as a harlot, confusing her with the woman who lived a sinful life and who washed Jesus' feet with her tears. But the gospels merely identify her as a woman suffering from demonic possession. After her deliverance, she became a devoted disciple of Jesus, traveling with him along with other of his followers, both male and female. Some scholars believe she may have been a leader in the early church. Her name is preserved in all four gospels, and she is also mentioned first in the list of women disciples presented in Luke 8:1–3 and first among the women mentioned in Mark 16:1.

Mary Magdalene was also the most prominent witness of Jesus' death, burial, and resurrection. Since women were not considered reliable witnesses in early first-century Israel, many scholars see this as more evidence of the veracity of the New Testament. They point out that no writer of that period would have willingly included such information unless it were true.

Though most of the disciples fled once Jesus was arrested and tried, Mary and many other women were with him at the crucifixion. As a woman who remained faithful to Jesus throughout his crucifixion, death, burial, and resurrection, she is a model of what it means to follow Jesus.

When the Romans crucified insurrectionists or criminals, they usually left their decaying bodies hanging on the cross to serve as a mark of shame and a crude warning to other malcontents. But it was Jewish practice to bury bodies on the day of death.

Ordinary people were buried in shallow pits while the wealthy were buried in family tombs carved from the rock. Generally these consisted of underground chambers accessed through a low entryway and sealed by a stone to keep animals out. The body was laid on a bench cut into the rock, anointed with oil and spices, and then wrapped in linen strips. The jaw may have been held in place by a separate piece of cloth that wrapped around the head, and the entire body may then have been wrapped in a shroud.

Among the Jews, as with many people, burial practices were extremely important. For a body to be left in the open rather than being honorably buried was considered shameful and tragic.

# THE TAKEAWAY

1. Mary's experience of Jesus presents a dramatic "before and after" story. How have your own encounters with Jesus changed your life? Comment on other "before and after" stories of people you know who have encountered Christ in a deep way.

2. Mary was devoted to Jesus. In your own words, describe what you think it means to be a follower of Christ?

3. What compelled Mary and the other women to stay at the cross? Do you think you would have had the strength to do the same?

4. When tragedy or difficulty strikes, we might be tempted to think that darkness is stronger than light. How have you experienced God in times of personal darkness?

5. Imagine that Jesus has just spoken your name as you stand weeping outside of his empty tomb. What does that feel like? How does this experience impact your understanding of who he is? Of who you are in relationship to him?

# Scripture Index

# Eve

HER NAME MEANS
*"Life-Giving" or "Mother of All Who Have Life"*

HER CHARACTER: She came into the world perfectly at peace with her God and with her husband, the only other person on the planet. She lived in Paradise, possessing every pleasure imaginable. She never knew the meaning of embarrassment, misunderstanding, hurt, estrangement, envy, bitterness, grief, or guilt until she listened to her enemy and began to doubt God.

HER SORROW: That she and her husband were banished from Paradise and the presence of God, and that her first son was a murderer and her second son his victim.

HER JOY: That she had once tasted Paradise, and that God had promised that her offspring would eventually destroy her enemy.

KEY SCRIPTURES: Genesis 1:26–31; 2–4

# *Monday*

### HER STORY

The woman stirred and stretched, her skin soft and supple as a newborn's. One finger, then another moved in gentle exploration of the ground that cradled her. She could feel a warmth filling her, tickling her throat as it tried to escape, spilling out in the strong, glad noise of laughter. She felt surrounded, as though by a thousand joys, and then a touch calmed her without diminishing her joy.

Her eyes opened to a Brightness, her ears to a Voice. And then a smaller voice, echoing an elated response: "This is now bone of my bones and flesh of my flesh; she shall be called 'woman,' for she was taken out of man." Adam took hold of her, and their laughter met like streams converging.

The man and the woman walked naked and unashamed in Paradise. No shadows filled Eden — no disorder, discord, or fear.

Then one day a serpent spoke to the woman. "Did God really say, 'You must not eat from any tree in the garden'? ... You will not surely die. For God knows that when you eat of it your eyes will be opened, and you will be like God, knowing good and evil."

The woman listened. She remembered the Brightness, the Voice of God that had filled her with joy. Could she really be like God? Pressed hard by desire, she took the fruit and then shared it with her husband. Suddenly darkness spread across Eden. It came, not from the outside but from within, filling the man and the woman with shadows, cravings, and misery. Order gave way to disorder, harmony to discord, trust to fear.

Soon Adam and Eve heard the sound of their Creator walking in the garden, and they hid. "Where are you, Adam?" God called.

"I heard you in the garden," Adam replied, "and I was afraid because I was naked; so I hid."

Sin had driven its wedge inside their hearts, and God banished them from Eden, pronouncing judgment first on the wily serpent that had tempted the woman and then on her and on her husband. To the serpent's curse he added this promise: "I will put enmity between you and the woman, and between your offspring and hers; he will crush your head, and you will strike his heel." To the woman, God said: "I will greatly increase your pains in childbearing; with pain you will give birth to children. Your desire will be for your husband, and he will rule over you."

Then God warned Adam that after a lifetime of hard labor, his strength would decrease until his body would finally be wrapped in the dust from which God had formed him. The curse of death fell suddenly upon the new world.

So Adam and his wife were forced to flee Paradise, and Adam named her Eve, because she would be the mother of all the living. But her firstborn, Cain, became a murderer, and her second son, Abel, his victim.

As the years passed, sorrow chased sorrow in the heart of the first woman, and the last we see of her we imagine her not as a creature springing fresh from the hand of God, but as a woman in anguish, giving birth to another child. Her skin now stretches like worn canvas across her limbs, her hands claw the stony ground, grasping for something to hold on to, for anything to ease her pain. She can feel the child inside, filling her, his body pressing for a way of escape. The cries of mother and child meet like streams converging. And Seth is born.

Finally, with her child cradled against her breast, relief begins to spread across Eve's face. With rest her hope returns; a smile forms, and then, finally, laughter rushes from her lips. Try as she might, she cannot stifle her joy. For she remembers the Brightness and the Voice and the promise God gave: Sooner or later, despite many griefs, her seed would crush the serpent. In the end, the woman would win.

# Tuesday

## HER LIFE AND TIMES

### CHILDBIRTH

*E*ve was the first woman to conceive a child, the first to harbor a fertilized egg in her womb. Did she understand the miracle taking place within her as her belly swelled and her child began to move? Did she know the wonder of love for a child yet unborn? The Bible doesn't give us those answers. But it does tell us that Eve recognized that life was in God's control. At Cain's birth she exclaimed, "*With the help of the LORD* I have brought forth a man" (Genesis 4:1).

God's judgment on Eve—"with pain you will give birth to children"—was no doubt exactly what Eve experienced in birthing this first child. It's the process we appropriately term *labor*. Eve likely bore the pain and went through the entire birth with only Adam's help.

Later, Hebrew women had the help of experienced midwives, who knew remedies for common delivery difficulties. Midwives' responsibilities after the birth included cutting the umbilical cord, washing the newborn, rubbing it with salt for cleansing, and then wrapping it in swaddling cloths.

The birth stool referred to in Exodus 1:16 was probably a low stool on which the mother-to-be squatted, allowing the force of gravity to aid in the birth process. The midwife and possibly other close relatives held the mother's hands to give comfort as well as stability as she bore down.

Women throughout the centuries have borne the results of Eve's sin. Their pain in childbearing unites them in a common bond of an experience shared. The experience is an unusual combination of the earthly and at the same time the unearthly. The pains, the panting, the mess and disorder connected with the birth of a child are of the earth, of Eve herself. But what is brought forth, and the bond experienced between the mother and the child, is unearthly, something only the Creator of life could forge.

# *Wednesday*

**Read Genesis 2:18–25.**

1. What needs does Adam have that only a woman can fulfill?

2. What does being "one flesh" in a marriage mean, both physically and spiritually?

**Read Genesis 3:1–24.**

3. As the serpent tries to tempt Eve, what desires and fears in her does he appeal to?

4. What desires and fears make you vulnerable to temptation?

5. When caught after her sin, how does Eve experience each of the following?

    Shame

    Blame

    Pain

# *Thursday*

## HER PROMISE

*E*mbedded in the very curse put on Eve for her sin is a wonderful promise. God promises her, and succeeding generations: You "will give birth to children" (Genesis 3:16). God's grace and mercy are marvelously evident, even when he's pronouncing his judgment. He promises that the human race will continue even as he announces that death will now be inevitable.

Throughout Scripture, God's grace is often most beautifully evident within his judgments. When the world was so full of sin that he had to destroy it, God's grace saved Noah and his family. When the Israelites rebelled so thoroughly that captivity was inevitable, God's grace promised restoration. While judgment fell on David for his sin with Bathsheba, God's grace gave them Solomon as a son and successor.

When you are at your lowest, on your knees before God's judgment, never forget that his grace is still at work. And that is truly amazing.

### Promises in Scripture

*From the fullness of his grace we have all received one blessing after another.*

—JOHN 1:16

*But where sin increased, grace increased all the more, so that, just as sin reigned in death, so also grace might reign through righteousness to bring eternal life through Jesus Christ our Lord.*

—ROMANS 5:20–21

# *Friday*

## HER LEGACY OF PRAYER

*So God created human beings in his own image, in the image of God he created them; male and female he created them.*

—GENESIS 1:27

REFLECT ON:    Genesis 2:15 – 25: 3.

PRAISE GOD:    Because he created you in his own image, making you a woman capable of reflecting his love, truth, strength, goodness, wisdom, and beauty.

OFFER THANKS:    That imbedded in God's judgment of Adam and Eve is the promise of a Redeemer who will crush the head of our enemy, the devil.

CONFESS:    Your own tendency to mar God's image in you by preferring your will to his.

ASK GOD:    To help you surrender your life, so that he can fulfill his purpose for creating you.

### Lift Your Heart

Find a peaceful setting, surrounded by the beauty of creation, to meditate on what life must have been like in the garden of Eden. Think about what your life would be like if you experienced peace in all your relationships, if you never suffered physical or emotional pain, if you were never confused or ashamed or guilty, if you always experienced God's love and friendship. Let your imagination run riot as it fills in the details of God's original intention for your life and for those you love.

Then consider this: You were made for paradise. The joys you taste now are infinitesimal compared to those that await you in heaven, for "no eye has seen, no ear has heard, no mind has conceived what God has prepared for those who love him" (1 Corinthians 2:9).

---

*Father, give me a greater understanding of your original plan for our world. Help me to envision its beauty so I might live with a constant awareness that you intend to restore paradise to all who belong to you. May I surrender every sin and every sorrow to you, trusting that you will fulfill your purpose for my life. In Jesus' name I pray. Amen.*

# Women of the Bible

## A One-Year Devotional Study

*Ann Spangler and Jean E. Syswerda*

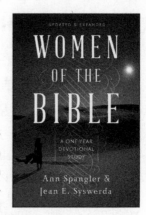

Bestselling, updated, and expanded devotional study, *Women of the Bible*, by Ann Spangler and Jean E. Syswerda, focuses on fifty-two remarkable women in Scripture — women whose struggles to live with faith and courage are not unlike your own.

Special features in Women of the Bible include:

- A list of all the women of the Bible
- Timeline of the women of the Bible
- A list of women in Jesus' family tree
- A list of women in Jesus' life and ministry

Vital and deeply human, the women in this book encourage you through their failures as well as their successes. You'll see how God acted in surprising and wonderful ways to draw them — and you — to himself.

This year-long devotional offers a unique method to help you slow down and savor the story of God's unrelenting love for his people, offering a fresh perspective that will nourish and strengthen your personal relationship with him.

*Available in stores and online!*

# Men of the Bible

## A One-Year Devotional Study of Men in Scripture

*Ann Spangler and Robert Wolgemuth*

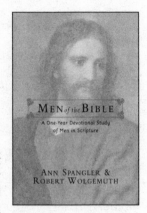

*Men of the Bible* takes a close-up look at fifty-two men in Scripture—complex flesh-and-blood characters whose strengths and weaknesses are similar to our own. Heroes and villains, sinners and prophets, commoners and kings, their dramatic life stories provide us with a fresh perspective on the unfolding story of redemption.

Though our culture differs vastly from the ones in which these fifty-two remarkable men lived, the fundamental issues we face remain the same. We still reach for great dreams and selfish ambitions. We wrestle with fear and indecision, struggle with sexual temptation, and experience the ache of loneliness and the devastation of betrayal. And, like many of these men, we long to walk more closely with the God who calls us into an intimate relationship with himself and who enables us to fulfill his purpose for our lives.

Designed for personal prayer and study or for use in small groups, *Men of the Bible* will help you make Bible reading a daily habit.

# Finding the Peace God Promises

*Ann Spangler*

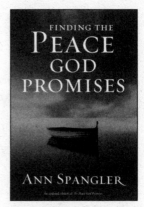

If God has promised to give us the "peace that passes understanding," why do we sometimes feel so anxious? What are we so afraid of? Are there ways of living that lead to peace? Conversely, are there ways of thinking and acting that lead to anxiety and a conflicted life?

*Finding the Peace God Promises* sets our longings for peace beside God's promise to provide it. Exploring the stories that shape us, the memories that define us, and the relationships that connect us, bestselling author Ann Spangler looks for ways to help readers experience a more peaceful life. With exercises that are easy to replicate and principles that are simple to understand, this book is for anyone feeling burdened by the challenges of life.

As you learn about rest and healing from Scripture, Jewish tradition, the Amish, and many others, you will discover what shalom really means. And you may be surprised by your ability to experience transformative peace, no matter your circumstances.

# Sitting at the Feet of Rabbi Jesus

## How the Jewishness of Jesus Can Transform Your Faith

*Ann Spangler and Lois Tverberg*

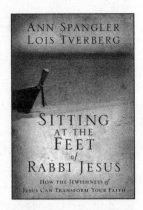

A rare chance to know Jesus as his first disciples knew him.

What would it be like to journey back to the first century and sit at the feet of Rabbi Jesus as one of his Jewish disciples? How would your understanding of the gospel have been shaped by the customs, beliefs, and traditions of the Jewish culture in which you lived?

*Sitting at the Feet of Rabbi Jesus* takes you on a fascinating tour of the Jewish world of Jesus, offering inspirational insights that can transform your faith. Ann Spangler and Lois Tverberg paint powerful scenes from Jesus' ministry, immersing you in the prayers, feasts, history, culture, and customs that shaped Jesus and those who followed him.

You will hear the parables as they must have sounded to first-century Jews, powerful and surprising. You will join the conversations that were already going on among the rabbis of his day. You will watch with new understanding as the events of his life unfold. And you will emerge with new excitement about the roots of your own Christian faith.

*Sitting at the Feet of Rabbi Jesus* will change the way you read Scripture and deepen your understanding of the life of Jesus. It will also help you to adapt the rich prayers and customs you learn about to your own life, in ways that both respect and enrich your Christian faith.

By looking at the Jewishness of Jesus, Ann Spangler and Lois Tverberg take you on a captivating journey into the heart of Judaism, one that is both balanced and insightful, helping you to better understand and appreciate your own faith.

*Available in stores and online!*

# Praying the Names of God

## A Daily Guide

*Ann Spangler, Bestselling Author of* Women of the Bible

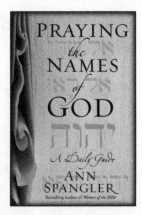

Mercy, protection, blessing—these are the concrete promises, the gifts that belong to everyone who loves God's name. *Praying the Names of God* will lead you into a fresh experience of God's love and power by exploring the Hebrew names of God revealed in Scripture and then showing you how to pray them on a daily basis. By praying these divine names and titles and by understanding the biblical context in which they were first revealed, you will gain a more intimate knowledge of God and his absolute faithfulness.

Ann Spangler identifies twenty-six of the most prominent names and titles of God, primarily drawn from the Hebrew Scriptures, to provide six-months' worth of devotions. Each new week will offer a deeper experience of God by leading you into a unique program of prayer and study.

Designed for personal prayer and study or for use in small groups, this unique devotional program will enable you to echo the psalmist's prayer: "Some trust in chariots and some in horses, but we trust in the name of the Lord our God."

*Available in stores and online!*

# Tender Words of God

## A Daily Guide

*Ann Spangler*

This daily guide to the Bible's most tender words will reshape your understanding of who God is and how he loves you.

Ann invites you to join her on this journey to know God better, to let his tender words become like guardians at the beginning and at the end of each day, convincing you once and for all of his faithful, committed love.

> *"If Jesus came to show us what God is really like, why doesn't learning about his life make us spend more time dancing in the street, hugging children, and feeding the poor? Finally— Ann Spangler has given focus to the positive words of life that, if we let them, will change everything."* —Gloria Gaither

> *"Ann Spangler has done it again—given us a fresh glimpse of God through his own words."* —John Ortberg